Living for a
Just Society

A Guided Discovery for Groups and Individuals

Kevin Perrotta

LOYOLAPRESS.
CHICAGO

LOYOLAPRESS.

3441 N. ASHLAND AVENUE
CHICAGO, ILLINOIS 60657
(800) 621-1008
WWW.LOYOLAPRESS.ORG

Nihil Obstat
Reverend John G. Lodge, S.S.L., S.T.D.
Censor Deputatus
August 13, 2004

Imprimatur
Most Reverend Raymond E. Goedert, M.A., S.T.L., J.C.L.
Vicar General
Archdiocese of Chicago
August 31, 2004

The *Nihil Obstat* and *Imprimatur* are official declarations that a book is free of doctrinal and moral error. No implication is contained therein that those who have granted the *Nihil Obstat* and *Imprimatur* agree with the content, opinions, or statements expressed.

The Scripture quotations contained herein are from the New Revised Standard Version Bible: Catholic Edition, copyright © 1993 and 1989 by the Division of Christian Education of the National Council of the Churches of Christ in the U.S.A. Used by permission. All rights reserved. Subheadings in Scripture quotations have been added by the author.

To James Cavnar, Paul and Gloria Melton, and George Mendenhall.

Interior design by Kay Hartmann/Communique Design
Illustration by Anni Betts

ISBN 0-8294-2063-0

Printed in the United States of America
05 06 07 08 09 10 Bang 10 9 8 7 6 5 4 3 2 1

Contents

How to Use This Guide

If you want to learn how to live according to God's vision for his people, the natural place to begin is the Bible. Because the Holy Spirit guided the authors of Scripture, the book they wrote is an always-fresh source of wisdom on everything concerning God and our relationship with him.

In this book we read a dozen or so selections from Scripture over the course of six weeks to learn about God's vision for justice in society and our role in his plans. As we proceed, we will explore connections between what we find in Scripture and our own life. The goal is to learn how to live in a way that moves us closer to God's purposes.

Our approach will be a *guided discovery*. It will be *guided* because we all need support in understanding Scripture and reflecting on what it means for our lives. Scripture was written to be understood and applied in the community of faith, so we read the Bible *for* ourselves but not *by* ourselves. Even if we are reading alone rather than in a group, we need resources that help us grow in understanding. Our approach is also one of *discovery,* because each of us needs to encounter Scripture for ourselves and consider its meaning for our life. No one can do this for us.

This book is designed to give you both guidance for understanding and tools for discovery.

The introduction on page 6 will guide your reading by providing background material and helping you get oriented to the subject of our exploration. Each week, a brief "Background"section will give you context for the reading, and the "Exploring the Theme" section that follows the reading will bring out the meaning of the Scripture passages. Supplementary material between sessions will offer further resources for understanding.

The main tool for discovery is the "Questions for Reflection and Discussion" section in each session. The first questions in this section are designed to spur you to notice things in the text, sharpen your powers of observation, and read for comprehension. Other questions suggest ways to compare the people, situations, and experiences in the biblical texts with your own life and the world today—an important step toward grasping what God is saying to you through the Scripture and what form your response might be. Choose the questions you think will work best for you. Preparing to answer all the questions ahead of time is highly recommended.

We suggest that you pay particular attention to the final question each week, labeled "Focus Question." This question points to an especially important issue about social justice raised by the reading. You may find it difficult to answer this focus question briefly. Do leave enough time for everyone in the group to discuss it!

Other sections encourage you to take an active approach to your Bible reading and discussion. At the start of each session, "Questions to Begin" will help you break the ice and start talk flowing. Often these questions are light and have only a slight connection to the reading. After each Scripture reading, there is a suggested time for a "First Impression." This gives you a chance to express a brief, initial, personal response to the text. Each session ends with a "Prayer to Close" that suggests a way of expressing your response to God.

How long are the discussion sessions? We've assumed you will have about an hour and twenty minutes. If you have less time, you'll find that most of the elements can be shortened somewhat.

Is homework necessary? You will get the most out of your discussions if you read the weekly material and prepare your answers to the questions in advance of each meeting. If participants are not able to prepare, read the "Exploring the Theme" sections aloud at the points where they appear.

What about leadership? You don't have to be an expert in the Bible to lead a discussion. Choose one or two people to act as discussion facilitators, and have everyone in the group read "Suggestions for Bible Discussion Groups" (page 92) before beginning.

Does everyone need a guide? a Bible? Everyone in the group will need their own copy of this book. It contains the biblical texts, so a Bible is not absolutely necessary—but each person will find it useful to have one. You should have at least one Bible on hand for your discussions. (See page 96 for recommendations.)

Before you begin, take a look at the suggestions for Bible discussion groups (page 92) or individuals (page 95).

S ocial justice: whatever it is—and opinions vary widely—it is not an easy subject for discussion. In the view of some, social justice is a vague abstraction, a subject too massive to get your arms around, a big yawn. For others, mentioning social justice seems like sending out invitations to an argument. We've all been in situations where some justice issue was knocked around like a hockey puck by battling teams of conservatives or liberals. Little seems to come from such contentions.

So what are we doing here, setting out on a six-week exploration of the Bible's teachings on social justice? Will we end up bored, angry, or frustrated? Perhaps we would do better to make a donation to the local food pantry—even volunteer to help out one morning a month—and leave it at that.

But if we care about the people who use the food pantry— and other neighbors who suffer injustices or live with unmet needs—it makes sense to step back, look at our society, and ask some questions. Who suffers injustice? Whose needs go unmet? What perpetuates these problems?

These questions lead to others. What standards should we use to measure how just our society is? What principles should guide us in relating to each other so as to make society better for everyone? Beyond these questions lie even more basic ones. Has God given us any vision for social life? What is God doing to bring justice in the world? How can we cooperate with him?

If we search the Bible, we will find that a great deal of light is shed on these issues. With the help of the Holy Spirit, we can learn a lot that will help us move our lives and our society closer to the justice God has in mind.

For all its difficulties, the subject of social justice is too important for us to ignore. If the Bible were a house, social justice would not be merely a spare room where a person might occasionally go to do some sewing or read a book. Social justice would be the great hall, the center of activity. Social justice, in fact, lies at the heart of God's vision for our lives.

In the biblical account, God initiates his great saving plan for humankind by calling Abraham. God's intention is that Abraham's descendants will "keep the way of the Lord by doing righteousness and justice" (Genesis 18:19). Later, through Moses, God instructs Abraham's descendants, the people of Israel, in a just way of life: "Justice, and only justice, you shall pursue" (Deuteronomy 16:20). Then God sends prophets to the Israelites, reminding them to "let justice roll down like waters, and righteousness like an ever-flowing stream" (Amos 5:24) and reproaching them for abandoning this way of life (just a list of citations would fill pages; start with Isaiah 5:7–9; Jeremiah 7:1–15; Amos 2:6–8). Finally, Jesus comes, the fulfillment of God's promise to send one who would bring "justice to victory" (Matthew 12:20).

Concern with social justice in the Bible is broader and more prevalent than may be apparent in our English translations. The English words that translators have at their disposal do not perfectly match the Hebrew, Aramaic, and Greek words in the original texts. Our English words *justice* and *judgment* carry the flavor of the courtroom; our words *righteous* and *righteousness* suggest individual integrity. Consequently, when we encounter *justice* and *judgment* in our Bibles, we tend to think of judicial affairs. *Right* and *righteousness* lead us to think of the individual person's virtue and relationship with God.

In some cases, these interpretations are perfectly correct. Exodus 23:2 has the courtroom in view: "When you bear witness in a lawsuit, you shall not side with the majority so as to pervert justice." Paul is speaking about the individual's status before God when he writes of "the free gift of righteousness" in Jesus Christ (Romans 5:17).

But consider Zechariah 7:9–10: "Render true judgments, show kindness and mercy to one another; do not oppress the widow, the orphan, the alien, or the poor." Biblical scholar Moshe Weinfeld points out that there is an apparent contradiction here, since "true judgments" in a court of law are unbiased even by "kindness and mercy" (see Leviticus 19:15). "However," Weinfeld explains, "Zechariah here is not referring to the correct execution of justice in court, but rather to . . . the restoration of equilibrium to the society by aiding the needy: the stranger, widow and orphan." Thus here and in many passages in the Bible, the words translated "justice" and "judgment" refer to protecting and supporting those who lack resources and power.

In the Bible, the words rendered "righteous" and "righteousness" often have a social rather than individual meaning. They refer to how people relate to one another. Righteousness means doing the right thing toward other people. Speaking about people who delight in God's commandments, the psalmist says, "They have distributed freely, they have given to the poor; their righteousness endures forever" (Psalm 112:9). Notice that the psalmist connects acting rightly with caring for the needy. The prophet Daniel makes the same connection when he gives the king of Babylon this advice: "Atone for your sins with righteousness, and your iniquities with mercy to the oppressed" (Daniel 4:27).

The Old Testament writers often link *justice* and *righteousness* (Genesis 18:19; Psalm 99:4; Jeremiah 23:5). Used in tandem, *justice* and *righteousness* mean more than treating everyone fairly under the law or delivering impartial judicial decisions. Jeremiah tells the king of Judah to "act with justice and righteousness" with this explanation: "Deliver from the hand of the oppressor anyone who has been robbed. And do no wrong or violence to the alien, the orphan, and the widow, or shed innocent blood" (Jeremiah 22:3). Together, *justice* and *righteousness* express a vision of social justice.

In the biblical view social justice involves putting an end to oppression, freeing those who are exploited, ensuring that people have what they need for a dignified and productive life, and opening the opportunity for everyone to make a constructive contribution to society. To seek social justice means more than making sure that everyone gets a fair trial. It means improving the conditions of poor people. "Put away violence and oppression, and do what is just and right. Cease your evictions of my people, says the Lord God" (Ezekiel 45:9).

The biblical concept of social justice, then, includes not only what we might call "strict justice" but also kindness and mercy. The biblical writers make this clear when they combine *justice* and *righteousness* with *mercy* and *love.* God "loves righteousness and justice; the earth is full of the steadfast love of the Lord"

(Psalm 33:5). "I act with steadfast love, justice, and righteousness in the earth, for in these things I delight, says the Lord" (Jeremiah 9:24). God tells his people, "I will take you for my wife in righteousness and in justice, in steadfast love, and in mercy" (Hosea 2:19).

Jesus embraces this tradition. His vision of social justice is the one expressed throughout the Old Testament: people dealing with one another fairly and honestly while showing mercy and compassion to those in need. When Jesus declares that those who "hunger and thirst for righteousness" will be happy (Matthew 5:6), he is referring to those who strive for both the personal rightness of a sin-free life and the rightness of a just society. He is declaring blessed those who seek a society like the one that Zechariah spoke of—where the poor and weak are freed from oppression and deprivation and everyone has access to an abundant and productive life.

The Bible does not present the ideal of social justice in a treatise on politics, economics, or law. Certainly there are laws and instructions in the Bible; they play a crucial role in communicating the ethos of social justice that we are discussing—as we will see in our readings in Week 2. But Scripture is basically a narrative. It is the account of God's act of creation, of his saving interactions with human beings, and of the final accomplishment of his intentions for us in his eternal kingdom. The Bible communicates its vision of social justice, and our obligations to pursue this vision, within the great story of God's activity.

The biblical story reveals God's original purposes for human society. It charts humanity's divergences from God and his purposes—and the painful consequences of diverging from God's plan—and chronicles God's continuous efforts to overcome the problems we humans have gotten ourselves into. God's efforts climaxed in the coming of his Son, Jesus Christ. The New Testament writers bear witness that Jesus' death and resurrection is the act through which God brings his wandering, diverging human creatures back to himself and initiates his ultimate project of restoring justice in society. In the end, Scripture reveals, God will bring forth a new creation, in which he will bring us into a condition of love for him and love for one another—the perfection of social justice. In the meantime, God summons and empowers us to reshape our lives and society to reflect his new creation, which he has already planted in our midst through Jesus' death and resurrection.

Our readings from Scripture over the next six weeks will give us a sense of the scope of God's plans for justice among us. The selected passages highlight God's initiatives, thus empha-sizing the fact that our part in contributing to social justice is to respond to what he is already doing.

God challenges us to become translators of the biblical story—not translators of words into words but of meanings into reality. Our task is to take hold of the principles and lessons communicated in the scriptural writings to people long ago and to bring them into our own situations today. For example, in portions of the Old Testament we find God's guidance for social justice given to the people of Israel at the time when they were peasants and shepherds in the centuries before Christ; in the New Testament we observe God inspiring efforts for social justice among the early Christians who constituted a network of little groups within the vast Roman Empire. It is up to us to learn from their experiences in their situations and to act in our very different modern world on what we have learned. What a just society might have looked like in the eleventh century BC or the first century AD is quite different from what it would look like today.

Our great resource for the task of translation is the Church. The Church is the living bridge between the world in which the Bible was written and the world in which we read the Bible. The Church provides us with a tradition of reflection on all that God has communicated to us in Scripture on the subject of social justice. And along with the tradition of reflection goes a tradition of application. In the history of the Church, we find countless examples of men and women who put the Bible's vision of social justice into action in their situations.

In the last century or so, in the face of rapid social change, the popes and bishops have updated and extended the Church's reflections on social justice. Their teaching on social justice helps us to discern the basic social-justice themes in Scripture and perceive the implications of the scriptural teaching for our modern world. To help us access this sizable body of modern teaching on social justice, the bishops in the United States have distilled its most important points. Seven themes, they have found, are fundamental. Here is their list (the quotations are from the bishops' 1990 statement, *A Century of Social Teaching: A Common Heritage, a Continuing Challenge*):

1. Because each human being is created in the image of God, "each person possesses a basic dignity that comes from God." Thus, "the test of every institution or policy is whether it enhances or threatens human life and human dignity."

2. "Each person has basic rights and responsibilities." Among the rights are religious freedom, the freedom to raise a family, and access to a share in the earth's goods—food, clothing, housing, health care, education—sufficient for a truly human life for oneself and one's family. Among the responsibilities is the simple duty "to work for the common good."

3. "The human person is . . . social." We naturally live in communities, most basically the family. Thus families deserve the support of society. We have a natural right and responsibility to cooperate in various kinds of political, professional, and voluntary associations.

4. "Work is an expression of our dignity and a form of continuing participation in God's creation." For this reason, "people have the right to decent and productive work, to decent and fair wages, to private property and economic initiative."

5. "Our tradition calls us to put the needs of the poor and vulnerable first." A basic yardstick for measuring the justice of our society, then, is the degree to which we aid those among us who have few resources and are less able to care for themselves.

6. "We are one human family." Consequently, we have a responsibility for each other's welfare. This is sometimes called the principle of solidarity.

7. God has entrusted the earth to our care, to be used in accord with his intentions, not simply for our own benefit. By caring for creation we show respect for the Creator.

Building on these basic themes, the Church identifies secondary principles. Many of them come in balanced pairs. For example:

◆ Private property is an important right, but property rights are not absolute. Possession is stewardship: we should always use our property for the common good.

◆ A free market in goods and services is beneficial because it allows many people to participate in building society and benefit from their own labors. The market, however, must be adjusted to prevent injustices and exploitation.

◆ People have the right to work together for justice. Thus, for example, labor unions are a legitimate means of achieving equity in the workplace. But in advancing our interests through associations, we should seek social harmony. So, staying with our example, unions should not regard management as an enemy but should strive for cooperation.

◆ Government has a positive role in eliminating certain injustices and meeting needs that cannot be met in any other way. But government should not do what individuals and groups can do for themselves.

Modern popes and bishops have applied these kinds of principles to a very wide variety of particular issues—the protection of life, education, health care, immigration, and so on.

The bishops' identification of key principles of social justice in the biblical tradition guided me in selecting the particular passages we will read in this book, in composing the "Exploring the Theme" sections, and in suggesting "Questions for Reflection and Discussion." As you make your way through the readings, refer back to the key principles of social justice that the bishops have identified in the biblical and Christian tradition. Going back and forth between the biblical texts and the Church's teaching is a very productive way of learning about social justice. In a small book, it has been possible to offer only a few introductory pointers to the immense Catholic tradition of reflection and action on the biblical vision of social justice. Hopefully your reflections and discussions will spur you to learn more about this tradition. For suggestions for further investigation, see "Resources" (page 96).

In six sessions we can only sample what the Bible has to say on social justice. But while our excerpts are few and short, they give us valuable insights into God's purposes. Through our readings, we can hear God speaking to us, challenging us to join him in the fulfillment of his purposes.

Oh, yes, what about arguments? On the subject of social justice, arguments are not inevitable, but it seems to me that disagreements are likely and are to be welcomed. The bishops at Vatican Council II (1962–65) made a distinction that is helpful to keep in mind if we wish to have healthy disagreement and avoid futile verbal battles. They wrote that "no one is permitted to identify the authority of the Church exclusively with his own opinion" (*The Church in the Modern World,* section 43). Thus the bishops distinguished between (a) the Bible and the Church's teaching and (b) the application of the Bible and Church teaching to particular situations. Problems arise if we present our opinions (b) as though they were the teaching of Scripture and the Church (a). But we can engage in useful discussions, and even disagreements, by affirming that we share a commitment to (a) and acknowledging each other's freedom to disagree about (b).

The bishops of the United States put this distinction into practice in their book *Economic Justice for All* (1986; reissued as *Tenth Anniversary Edition of Economic Justice for All*). In the first part of the book they examine (a) Scripture and the basic principles of Catholic social teaching. Then they suggest (b) ways that the teaching might be applied to American society. The bishops point out the difference between the authoritative teaching section of their book and their proposed applications. They write: "We know that some of our specific recommendations are controversial. As bishops, we do not claim to make these prudential judgments with the same kind of authority that marks our declarations of principle. . . . There are . . . many specific points on which men and women of good will may disagree. We look for a fruitful exchange among differing viewpoints."

Amen. Have great discussions. Then move from talking to acting. Check out the organizations mentioned in "Resources" (page 96). Get connected!

HUMANS: A MARVELOUS GROUP

Questions to Begin

10 minutes
Use a question or two to get warmed up for the reading.

1 Name something you always like to begin. Name something you never like to begin.

2 When have you made something you would describe as very good?

Christ is now at work in the hearts of men by the power of his Spirit; not only does he arouse in them a desire for the world to come but he quickens, purifies, and strengthens the generous aspirations of mankind to make life more human and conquer the earth for this purpose.

The Pope and Bishops of the Catholic Church at Vatican Council II, 1965, *The Church in the Modern World* (section 38)

10 minutes
Read the biblical passages aloud. Let individuals take turns reading paragraphs.

The Background

With sea monsters and symbolic trees, the first chapters of the Bible seem a far cry from the issues we face in the modern world. But using imagery from their own time, the authors of Genesis communicated an important message for every age. Quite simply, God created all. Therefore, everything belongs to him. Everything we have is on loan from God; we ourselves are tenants in his world. In every age it is easy to lose sight of these basic truths. Yet these are the starting points for understanding how we ought to live with one another.

The Reading: Genesis 1:1–5, 9–13, 20–31; 2:4–5, 7–9, 15–25

God Creates Almost Everything

1:1 In the beginning when God created the heavens and the earth, 2 the earth was a formless void and darkness covered the face of the deep, while a wind from God swept over the face of the waters. 3 Then God said, "Let there be light"; and there was light. 4 And God saw that the light was good; and God separated the light from the darkness. 5 God called the light Day, and the darkness he called Night. And there was evening and there was morning, the first day. . . .

9 And God said, "Let the waters under the sky be gathered together into one place, and let the dry land appear." And it was so. 10 God called the dry land Earth, and the waters that were gathered together he called Seas. And God saw that it was good. 11 Then God said, "Let the earth put forth vegetation: plants yielding seed, and fruit trees of every kind on earth that bear fruit with the seed in it." And it was so. 12 . . . And God saw that it was good. 13 And there was evening and there was morning, the third day. . . .

20 And God said, "Let the waters bring forth swarms of living creatures, and let birds fly above the earth across the dome of the sky." 21 So God created the great sea monsters and every living creature that moves, of every kind, with which the waters swarm, and every winged bird of every kind. And God saw that it was good. 22 God blessed them, saying, "Be fruitful and multiply and fill the

waters in the seas, and let birds multiply on the earth." 23 And there was evening and there was morning, the fifth day.

24 And God said, "Let the earth bring forth living creatures of every kind: cattle and creeping things and wild animals of the earth of every kind." And it was so. 25 God made the wild animals of the earth of every kind, and the cattle of every kind, and everything that creeps upon the ground of every kind. And God saw that it was good.

God Completes His Creation

26 Then God said, "Let us make humankind in our image, according to our likeness; and let them have dominion over the fish of the sea, and over the birds of the air, and over the cattle, and over all the wild animals of the earth, and over every creeping thing that creeps upon the earth."

27 So God created humankind in his image,
    in the image of God he created them;
    male and female he created them.

28 God blessed them, and God said to them, "Be fruitful and multiply, and fill the earth and subdue it; and have dominion over the fish of the sea and over the birds of the air and over every living thing that moves upon the earth." 29 God said, "See, I have given you every plant yielding seed that is upon the face of all the earth, and every tree with seed in its fruit; you shall have them for food. 30 And to every beast of the earth, and to every bird of the air, and to everything that creeps on the earth, everything that has the breath of life, I have given every green plant for food." And it was so. 31 God saw everything that he had made, and indeed, it was very good.

Man and Woman in a Garden

2:4 . . . In the day that the LORD God made the earth and the heavens, 5 when no plant of the field was yet in the earth and no herb of the field had yet sprung up . . . 7 . . . the LORD God formed man from the dust of the ground, and breathed into his nostrils the breath of life; and the man became a living being. 8 And the LORD God planted a garden in Eden, in the east; and there he put the man whom he had formed. 9 Out of the ground the LORD God made to grow every tree that is pleasant to the sight and good for food, the tree of life also in the midst of the garden, and the tree of the knowledge of good and evil. . . .

15 The LORD God took the man and put him in the garden of Eden to till it and keep it. 16 And the LORD God commanded the man, "You may freely eat of every tree of the garden; 17 but of the tree of the knowledge of good and evil you shall not eat, for in the day that you eat of it you shall die."

18 Then the LORD God said, "It is not good that the man should be alone; I will make him a helper as his partner." 19 So out of the ground the LORD God formed every animal of the field and every bird of the air, and brought them to the man to see what he would call them; and whatever the man called every living creature, that was its name. 20 The man gave names to all cattle, and to the birds of the air, and to every animal of the field; but for the man there was not found a helper as his partner. 21 So the LORD God caused a deep sleep to fall upon the man, and he slept; then he took one of his ribs and closed up its place with flesh. 22 And the rib that the LORD God had taken from the man he made into a woman and brought her to the man. 23 Then the man said,

"This at last is bone of my bones
and flesh of my flesh;
this one shall be called Woman,
for out of Man this one was taken."

24 Therefore a man leaves his father and his mother and clings to his wife, and they become one flesh. 25 And the man and his wife were both naked, and were not ashamed.

First Impression

5 minutes
Briefly mention a question you have about the reading or one thing in it that surprised, impressed, delighted, or challenged you. No discussion! Just listen to one another's reactions.

Exploring the Theme

If participants have not read this section already, read it aloud. Otherwise go on to "Questions for Reflection and Discussion."

Genesis 1:1–25. Ah, the excitement, as God brings up the lights in the universe for the first time!

The Israelite sages who wrote this creation account shaped it to carry a message that went against the views of their Near Eastern neighbors. Neighboring peoples believed that at the beginning of time gods fought each other, and from this combat the heavens and the earth came into existence. The biblical authors excluded anything of this sort. In Genesis, there is no struggle between gods, because there is only one God. He calls everything into existence with a series of solemn edicts.

Israel's neighbors regarded the heavenly bodies and the forces of nature as manifestations of the divine. In a sense, they worshiped thunderstorms, sea monsters, rivers, and fertility. Sun, Moon, Sea, Grain, and Plague were gods in the ancient Near East. The authors of Genesis, however, show a universe swept clean of nature deities. The authors do not even use the words *sun* and *moon* (1:14–19). The fertility of nature, demoted from divine status, is shown to be a gift of God (1:9–13, 22). There may be sea monsters somewhere out there in the deep (1:21), but they are not deities—just something God likes to have in his oceans (compare the sea monster Leviathan in Psalm 104:24–26).

Unlike ancient Near Eastern peoples who saw a universe crowded with gods, we modern people tend to view the universe without God. For us, the vital message of Genesis is that the universe is no mere expanse of matter and energy but a *creation.* It is not a neutral field on which we can play whatever games we like, but a workshop for accomplishing the Creator's purposes, a symphony hall for playing his music.

Genesis 1:26–2:25. Finally comes humankind. We are so important that the inspired authors provide two accounts of our creation. The second account does not follow the first account chronologically but stands beside it. Both accounts emphasize our place of honor, but in opposite ways. In the first account (1:26–31), we come onstage last, as the high point of creation (note the kind of drumroll in 1:26 that precedes our entrance). In the second account (2:4–25), God makes us first, as a sign of our precedence; animals follow in subordinate position.

The whole universe reflects God's power and wisdom. Sun and moon, rivers and mountains, fruit trees and the birds singing in them—all display God's goodness. But the part of creation that best shows what God is like is the human race, for we alone are created in his image and likeness (1:26–27). Our entire being— body, spirit, mind, freedom, capacity to love—reflects the Creator. And God has made us like himself so that we might live in a unique relationship with him.

In the ancient Near East, the king was considered to be "the image of god." By declaring that the entire human race is the image of God (1:26–27), Genesis asserts that not just one man but all men and women have royal status. The human race is a royal family, each of us a princess or a prince. Together we play a kingly role on earth, ruling on behalf of our Creator. Early Christian teachers such as Gregory of Nyssa and John Chrysostom declared that God prepared the earth as palace and throne for humanity.

Human rule is very strongly expressed: the Hebrew word translated "subdue" (1:28) means "subjugate." This emphasizes God's delegation of authority to us, but it does not suggest that God authorizes us to treat the earth in an arbitrary, selfish way. God has brought a *good* universe into existence (1:4, 12, 18, 21, 25), and he does not intend for us to mess it up. Our rule is to be modeled on his rule, which is life-giving and appreciative of the beauty of his subjects. God places us in the world not as marauders but as stewards. We are to discover and nurture the good that he has built into it.

The second human creation account also expresses our superiority over earth's other creatures. The man's nose is the only one into which God breathes life (2:7). The man names the animals (2:19–20), a sign of dominance that imitates and completes what his divine father began (1:5, 8, 10). The fact that none of the animals can serve as companion underlines the man's distinctiveness.

The second account, too, expresses our role in the world, using not royal but agricultural imagery. God puts the man in a "garden"—the Hebrew word means an enclosed orchard of fruit trees—to care for it (2:15). Humanity is given work to do. The man's assignment, to tend the trees so they bear fruit, symbolizes our responsibility to bring forth the potential that God has placed within the earth. The goodness of creation will become manifest through what people do with it.

God's human masterpiece is incomplete until man and woman stand facing each other. God creates the woman to be a "helper as his partner" for the man (2:18, 20). The term "helper" brings out the practical side of the relationship: she will help him— and he will help her—in the necessities of everyday life. The term "partner" means that the man and the woman are genuine counterparts. They correspond to each other sexually. In fact, they are so perfectly suited for each other that when they join together, they become as one (2:24). Seeing the woman for the first time, the man echoes his Creator: "This one is very good indeed!" (See 2:23; compare 1:4, 12, 18, 21, 25.) The human race is off to a fabulous start.

Reflections. The creation accounts have a lot to say about social justice. Here it is possible to consider only a few points.

Environment. As human mastery over the earth increases, the message that God wishes us to tend the earth (2:15) increases in importance. Earth is *God's.* Taking care of it is not simply a nice thing to do or merely a wise thing to do for ourselves and future generations; it is a sacred responsibility. And each of us shares in this responsibility, since we all acquire and use and dispose of the things of earth. We are all called to learn about and cherish the earth—and to keep ecological issues in mind as we advocate policies and elect government officials.

Person. The creation accounts provide the foundational principle on which any just society is constructed: the supreme dignity of each human being. God created humankind in his own image and likeness—and in his image and likeness he continues to create each human individual. "For it was you who formed my inward parts; you knit me together in my mother's womb" (Psalm 139:13). God is the light for which every human person is created (John 1:9). Of course, we receive life through our parents, but God is directly involved in this transmission of life. Each of us is a creation of God, whether we originated in an act of love between husband and wife or through rape or casual sex or any other way. A loving God has brought each of us into existence for himself.

Consequently, to deliberately take an innocent human life is the most serious violation of God's purposes. To kill a human being is to destroy God's creative masterpiece. Taking a human life, except when it is necessary in order to defend life against an unjust aggressor, is an attack on God who created that life as a reflection of himself. From first moment to last, the life of each human being is infinitely precious to God as a unique reflection of his infinite goodness.

Work. Created in God's image, we share in his ongoing activity in the world. By our labor, we are "unfolding the creator's work," the bishops stated at Vatican Council II (1962–65). Each of us has an innate desire and capacity to take part in the ruling and tending of earth that God has entrusted to humanity. We work not only to support ourselves and our families but to play our small part in God's great purpose as the human race unfolds the possibilities that he has hidden in his world.

Working is part of our dignity, Pope John Paul II says. It is good for us even when it is hard, he points out, because through work it is possible to achieve "fulfillment as a human being and indeed in a sense become 'more a human being'" (*On Human Work*, section 9). The pope notes that each of us wishes to have a place, and even a sense of ownership, at the "great workbench" at which the whole human race is laboring (section 14). Thus, access to work is part of social justice. A just society helps individuals overcome the obstacles of location or lack of training or disability that might keep them from employment. And it ensures appropriate working conditions for all who bear God's image.

Questions for Reflection and Discussion

45 minutes
Choose questions according to your interest and time.

1 Why is tending fruit trees (2:15) a good symbol for the work that God gives the human race to do?

2 What might be the significance of the woman's being formed from the rib of the man (2:21–22)?

3 After 2:23, what do you suppose the man and the woman talked about?

4 Identify one social practice that seems in harmony with our responsibility for the environment and one that doesn't. Identify one law that seems in harmony with our responsibility for the natural environment and one that doesn't. Is it possible to be black-and-white in making such judgments? What sorts of complexities have to be considered in deciding whether practices and laws should be changed to better care for the environment?

5 What experience has helped you see the value of each person's life even when a person is not yet born or is sick, feeble, disabled, in pain, or close to death? Has the experience led you to change anything in your life?

6 What injustices are sometimes suffered by people who are unborn, disabled, sick, or dying? What can be done to protect them?

7 What is the role of work in God's purposes for your life? What has helped you realize the importance of work in the process of attaining maturity?

8 Are there types of work that do not fit the dignity of human beings? What about working conditions? What is one thing that could be done to alleviate a current problem in this area?

9 **Focus Question.** How does the belief that God created everything affect the way one views human life? the way one views work? the way one views the natural environment?

Prayer to Close

10 minutes
Use this approach—or create your own!

◆ Pray Psalm 8 or Psalm 104 as a
thanksgiving for God's creation
of the universe and especially of
the human race. End with an
Our Father as a prayer asking
God to guide and help you put
into practice any decisions you
have reached through your
reflection and discussion.

Saints in the Making

Young, Globally Minded, and Outspoken

This section is a supplement for individual reading.

If you happen to attend a conference on development sponsored by the United Nations or the European Union, you may run into a lively group of teens and young adults called the World Youth Alliance (WYA). The WYA got started in 1999 with a small band of young people who took part in a UN conference in New York, where they promoted respect for life against a proabortion agenda. A young Catholic from Canada, Anna Halpine, founded the group. Over the next five years, the WYA grew into an organization counting a million members in a hundred countries, including the United States and Canada.

The organization trains members to participate in UN and EU conferences. But most members are active at the local level. The WYA organizes reading groups and sponsors Culture of Life events that include art exhibits, musical concerts, and videos on children and family life, as well as photography, hiking, bicycling, and even ballroom dancing. The alliance provides training and a network of support for young people who want to take political action in their own countries.

At a youth meeting organized by the UN in New York in 2000, where some delegates argued that minors should have access to contraceptives and abortion without parental consent, the WYA spoke up for a different kind of development: improvement in housing, education, and health care. The following year, a WYA representative told a session of the UN General Assembly that "stable, loving families are the only assurance for the full development of the child. It is only within a nurturing and protective framework that the child can learn to build a civilization of love."

Against international policies relying on population control to deal with environmental problems, the WYA argues that valuing people and valuing the environment go hand in hand. At a UN conference in 2002, the WYA declared: "Responsible stewardship means we view each person as a precious and vital resource of great potential, capable of answering the challenges societies face with innovation and invention. The creativity of human beings is the earth's greatest resource."

Between Discussions

Nice Start, Poor Follow-through

As we all know, the first human beings did not cooperate with God's plans. After creation came the Fall.

God designed human beings for satisfying work, harmonious marriage and social life, earthly abundance, and immunity to death—an immunity symbolized by access to "the tree of life" in the garden where he placed the first couple (Genesis 2:9). But the first man and woman felt that God's purposes were restrictive. They aspired to define their own destiny, to set their own moral standards, to attain knowledge and control beyond their lot. This is expressed somewhat symbolically in the chapter of Genesis following our reading in Week 1. With the hope of becoming like God (Genesis 3:5), the man and the woman eat from "the tree of the knowledge of good and evil," which God had told them to avoid (Genesis 3:6; compare 2:9, 17). This act of pride, disobedience, and distrust of God's goodness results in their expulsion from the garden. Cut off from the tree of life, they no longer have a remedy for the forces of degeneration and death.

The rupture in humans' relationship with God distorts their relationships with one another. The man and the woman fall into patterns of lust and shame, domination and subservience (Genesis 3:7, 16). Among their children and descendents, envy, murder, and vengefulness appear (Genesis 4:3–8, 23–24). In addition, human harmony with the natural environment is disrupted, throwing economic life out of whack and setting the stage for conflict over natural resources and human labor (Genesis 3:17–19). As technology develops and cities grow, so do arrogance, injustice, and violence (Genesis 4:17–24; 6:5–13; 11:1–9). The human world assumes the form in which we know it today—an arena where competing individuals and groups use power against each other for selfish ends.

Scripture testifies that God did not abandon human beings or his vision of social justice and abundant human living. The Bible does not relate all the mysterious ways that God made himself known to men and women for countless millennia (but see Acts 14:16–17; 17:22–28) but focuses on his central plan for achieving his intentions for the human race. This plan involved a particular family and lineage in the ancient Near East—the descendants of a wandering shepherd couple named Abraham and Sarah (Genesis 12–50).

God's aim was to build a new society marked by justice. In this renewed society, people would recognize the dignity of individuals. The weak and needy would be freed from exploitation and would be given the wherewithal for a useful life. Society would be held together not so much by the force of law as by a sense of solidarity, fairness, and compassion. Moral instruction and training would form young people's consciences and guide them to shoulder their social responsibilities. In this new society, customs would curb the concentration of power and wealth by the few. The self-serving use of power by human kings would be abolished: God alone would be recognized as king.

The opportunity for actually bringing this new society into existence appeared when the descendants of Abraham and Sarah fell under a particularly oppressive regime in Egypt. The Egyptians enslaved them and subjected them to a policy of genocide. But God rescued them from this appalling situation (Exodus 1–15; this is probably in the thirteenth century before Christ). After rescuing the people, God proposed a new relationship to them. He would be their king, and they would learn to live as his new society. They accepted this covenant and undertook to follow the pattern of life that he gave them. Thus the people of Israel came into existence (Exodus 19–40).

At first, Israel was a community of shepherds and small farmers held together by this covenant with God and the way of life he had given them. They were a federation of tribes, without a human king or even a centralized government (twelfth and eleventh centuries before Christ).

In a sense, the Israelites were God's pilot project for the restoration of human society. They demonstrated what social justice would look like under the circumstances of rural life in the ancient Near East. Our next readings give us samples of the instructions for social life that God gave them.

ISRAEL: GOD'S PILOT PROJECT

Questions to Begin

10 minutes
Use a question or two to get warmed up for the reading.

1 When have you been glad to get a second chance to make a fresh start?

2 When have you lent something, knowing you might not get it back?

It is what a man is, rather than what he has, that counts. Technical progress is of less value than advances towards greater justice, wider brotherhood, and a more humane social environment. Technical progress may supply the material for human advance, but it is powerless to actualize it.

The Pope and Bishops of the Catholic Church at Vatican Council II, 1965, *The Church in the Modern World* (section 35)

10 minutes
Read the biblical passages aloud. Let individuals take turns
reading paragraphs.

The Background

After rescuing the Israelites from slavery in Egypt (Exodus 1–15),
God leads them through the dry, rocky terrain of the Sinai Peninsula
to a mountain where they camp for some time. Here God reveals
himself to them through their leader, Moses, and gives them instructions for the way of life they are to follow as a people bound in covenant to him and to one another. God intends the Israelites to be a
kind of pilot project for the restoration of justice in human society.
Our readings present excerpts from these instructions.

The Reading: Leviticus 19:1–3, 9–10, 13–18, 27–28, 32–36; Deuteronomy 15:1, 7–10, 12–15; Leviticus 25:10, 23–25, 28, 35–43

Honoring God, Loving One's Neighbor

Leviticus 19:1 The LORD spoke to Moses, saying:

2 Speak to all the congregation of the people of Israel and say
to them: You shall be holy, for I the LORD your God am holy. 3 You
shall each revere your mother and father, and you shall keep my
sabbaths: I am the LORD your God. . . .

9 When you reap the harvest of your land, you shall not reap to
the very edges of your field, or gather the gleanings of your harvest.
10 You shall not strip your vineyard bare, or gather the fallen grapes
of your vineyard; you shall leave them for the poor and the alien: I
am the LORD your God. . . .

13 You shall not defraud your neighbor; you shall not steal; and
you shall not keep for yourself the wages of a laborer until morning.
14 You shall not revile the deaf or put a stumbling block before the
blind; you shall fear your God: I am the LORD.

15 You shall not render an unjust judgment; you shall not be
partial to the poor or defer to the great: with justice you shall judge your
neighbor. 16 You shall not go around as a slanderer among your people,
and you shall not profit by the blood of your neighbor: I am the LORD.

17 You shall not hate in your heart anyone of your kin; you
shall reprove your neighbor, or you will incur guilt yourself. 18 You

shall not take vengeance or bear a grudge against any of your people, but you shall love your neighbor as yourself: I am the LORD. . . .

27 You shall not round off the hair on your temples or mar the edges of your beard. 28 You shall not make any gashes in your flesh for the dead or tattoo any marks upon you: I am the LORD. . . .

32 You shall rise before the aged, and defer to the old; and you shall fear your God: I am the LORD.

33 When an alien resides with you in your land, you shall not oppress the alien. 34 The alien who resides with you shall be to you as the citizen among you; you shall love the alien as yourself, for you were aliens in the land of Egypt: I am the LORD your God.

35 You shall not cheat in measuring length, weight, or quantity. 36 You shall have honest balances, honest weights, an honest ephah, and an honest hin: I am the LORD your God, who brought you out of the land of Egypt.

Forgiving Debts, Releasing Slaves

Deuteronomy 15:1 Every seventh year you shall grant a remission of debts. . . .

7 If there is among you anyone in need, a member of your community in any of your towns within the land that the LORD your God is giving you, do not be hard-hearted or tight-fisted toward your needy neighbor. 8 You should rather open your hand, willingly lending enough to meet the need, whatever it may be. 9 Be careful that you do not entertain a mean thought, thinking, "The seventh year, the year of remission, is near," and therefore view your needy neighbor with hostility and give nothing; your neighbor might cry to the LORD against you, and you would incur guilt. 10 Give liberally and be ungrudging when you do so, for on this account the LORD your God will bless you in all your work and in all that you undertake. . . .

12 If a member of your community, whether a Hebrew man or a Hebrew woman, is sold to you and works for you six years, in the seventh year you shall set that person free. 13 And when you send a male slave out from you a free person, you shall not send him out empty-handed. 14 Provide liberally out of your flock, your threshing floor, and your wine press, thus giving to him some of the bounty with which the LORD your God has blessed you. 15 Remember that you were a slave in the land of Egypt, and the LORD your God redeemed you. . . .

Cushioning the Poor from Adversities

Leviticus 25:10 And you shall hallow the fiftieth year and you shall proclaim liberty throughout the land to all its inhabitants. It shall be a jubilee for you: you shall return, every one of you, to your property and every one of you to your family. . . .

23 The land shall not be sold in perpetuity, for the land is mine; with me you are but aliens and tenants. 24 Throughout the land that you hold, you shall provide for the redemption of the land.

25 If anyone of your kin falls into difficulty and sells a piece of property, then the next of kin shall come and redeem what the relative has sold. . . . 28 But if there is not sufficient means to recover it, what was sold shall remain with the purchaser until the year of jubilee; in the jubilee it shall be released, and the property shall be returned. . . .

35 If any of your kin fall into difficulty and become dependent on you, you shall support them. . . . 36 Do not take interest in advance or otherwise make a profit from them, but fear your God; let them live with you. 37 You shall not lend them your money at interest taken in advance, or provide them food at a profit. 38 I am the LORD your God, who brought you out of the land of Egypt, to give you the land of Canaan, to be your God.

39 If any who are dependent on you become so impoverished that they sell themselves to you, you shall not make them serve as slaves. 40 They shall remain with you as hired or bound laborers. They shall serve with you until the year of the jubilee. 41 Then they and their children with them shall be free from your authority; they shall go back to their own family and return to their ancestral property. 42 For they are my servants, whom I brought out of the land of Egypt; they shall not be sold as slaves are sold. 43 You shall not rule over them with harshness, but shall fear your God.

First Impression

5 minutes
Briefly mention a question you have about the reading or one thing in it that surprised, impressed, delighted, or challenged you. No discussion! Just listen to one another's reactions.

Exploring the Theme

If participants have not read this section already, read it aloud. Otherwise go on to "Questions for Reflection and Discussion."

Congratulations: you're reading Leviticus! Supposedly Leviticus is the dullest book in the Bible. But perhaps it's not so boring after all?

Leviticus 19. This chapter is a grab bag of different laws, but all are concerned with developing a just society. The term used, however, is not *social justice* but *holiness.* God wants his people to be "holy" (19:2).

Holy means set apart. God is holy—absolutely set apart, absolutely different from creation. Things that belong to God in a special way are also holy. For most people in the ancient Near East, holiness has to do with ritual matters: temples, priests, and so on. The Israelites share this concept of holy persons, places, and things but add a deeper concept: holiness concerns behavior that reflects God's character. Here, for example, along with a command to guard against working on the sabbath (a ritual matter) goes a command to care for one's parents (a moral duty—19:3). Prohibitions against pagan rituals (19:27–28) are surrounded by expressions of the Golden Rule (19:18, 34). In the vision of the authors of Leviticus, a holy society is one where people *both* worship God in the temple *and* do what is right and good for others. Among the specifics for holy living:

19:9–10. Every farmer should leave a strip of his field unharvested. During harvesting, workers should not go back to pick up grain they drop or overlook. In the vineyard, small clusters of grapes should be left on the vine, and fallen fruit should be left on the ground. All this food is left for the poor. The underlying logic is this: holy behavior means treating reverently what belongs to God in a special way; caring for poor people is holy behavior; poor people, then, must belong to God in a special way (compare Matthew 25:31–46).

19:13. Day laborers lead a precarious existence. Even slaves have more economic security. A man working for a daily wage needs his pay at the end of his shift so his wife can buy bread the next day. So pay him today!

19:14. Treat the disabled with dignity. They, too, belong to God in a special way.

19:15. Render judicial decisions impartially. Although society should go out of its way to help its poorer members, no one, not even the poor, should receive favoritism in court.

19:17–18. Do not take vengeance; don't even desire it. Want and do what is good for your neighbor. This is holiness in a nutshell.

19:33–34. Don't love only the members of your group ("your people"—19:18). Love strangers, too. Leave their property alone and give them their legal rights. This concern for foreigners in a legal code is unique in the ancient Near East.

The inspired authors regard holiness as a goal not only for religious professionals like priests but for everyone. Everyone plays a part in society's becoming holy, that is, just. The child showing respect for an old person (19:32), the employee putting aside a grudge against her employer (19:18), the farmer leaving some of his barley crop for his poor neighbors (19:9), the woman using honest measures when she sells her olive oil in the market (19:35–36), the jurors giving a fair verdict (19:15)—all are contributing to social justice.

Leviticus 19 points us toward our responsibility for one another. This makes sense because we are a family, all descended from the same parents (Genesis 2). Thus no one should seem unimportant to us, no matter how different or far from us. In theory, this human solidarity is an ordinary thing. In practice, as we know, it is quite remarkable.

Deuteronomy 15. Most people in the ancient Near East work in agriculture. Many are small landowners with few reserves. If the weather or the market goes against them, they are forced to borrow money for food and seed. With interest rates at 20 percent or higher, loans are hard to repay. The loans are secured with the small farmers' lands and their family members, so nonpayment results in their losing their lands and their freedom. Once they lose their property and become slaves of large landowners, they have no way of regaining their former situation, no matter how hard they try. Given these dynamics, the social chasm between rich and poor tends to widen.

At the beginning of their reigns, some Mesopotamian and Egyptian kings cancel debts and liberate those held in debt slavery. Freed slaves can go home and reclaim their land. These proclamations of release add greatly to the kings' popularity. Deuteronomy 15 mandates a release of this kind. But for the Israelites, God is king. Thus in Israelite society, it is God who cancels debts and releases slaves. And his release occurs on a regular cycle (15:1), not at times chosen by human kings to enhance their prestige. God's approach to society benefits the poor, not the powerful.

For the Israelites, the regular release of slaves and debts is an experience of God's reign. God's invisible kingdom becomes visible through the wealthy members of society implementing the "remission" that he has proclaimed.

Leviticus 25. Beneath the laws in this chapter lies a fundamental principle: the Israelite people and their land belong to God (25:23, 42). God wants them to use his land to build a society where everyone has the basic requirements for a dignified life. Since stable family life is essential for building such a society, and, in the ancient Near East, stable family life requires property for farming and pasturing, God's policy is that each family should have its own property and the property should stay in the family. The goal is that large landowners will not gobble up small land holdings—and their owners. Chapter 25 presents means for achieving this goal:

◆ Since the people belong to God, they cannot become the property of anyone else (25:42). They can be bound to service, but only for a time.

◆ Land cannot be sold outright. Sales, in effect, are leases (25:23). The purchaser must sell the land back to the original owner if that owner or one of his relatives acquires the means to redeem it (25:24).

◆ Every fifty years, slaves and debts are released (25:10). This is called the "jubilee." (Why it is every fifty years here but every seven years in Deuteronomy 15 is a matter of scholarly debate.)

God once rescued his people from slavery in Egypt; now they must ensure freedom in the community (25:38). Just as God gave the Israelites a fresh start by bringing them out of Egypt, they should give each other a fresh start periodically by releasing debts and slaves. They are to act toward one another as God has acted toward them. Thus God continues to provide freedom and land to his people by instructing the more affluent members of the community to care for those who are poor and vulnerable.

Reflections. Our readings remind us of how many elements go into making a society just: cultural practices that benefit the needy, integrity in the judicial system, virtues such as honesty, even common courtesy. Many of these elements lie outside the sphere of government. The state can force owners to release slaves (Deuteronomy 15:12) but it cannot enforce a command to be generous toward those they release (Deuteronomy 15:12–15). Government officials can certify the weights and scales in the market (Leviticus 19:35–36) but cannot prevent meanness to deaf people or grudge bearing (Leviticus 19:14, 17–18). A just society requires just citizens.

Our readings are part of the educational program for developing the citizens needed for a just society. These Old Testament writings are in the form of laws, but they function more as instructions; they are material for a lifelong course in character formation. A just society, for example, requires citizens who feel compassion for those in need; so our readings cultivate compassion by reminding the people how merciful God was to their ancestors and by appealing to them to express their thankfulness for God's kindness by showing kindness to those in need. Because the Israelites know what it is like to be strangers and slaves in a foreign land, they should not harm foreigners and slaves in their own land (Leviticus 19:34; Deuteronomy 15:15). The laws in these readings are designed less as legal prescriptions than as an appeal to conscience.

In every society, the basic training ground for citizens of character and conscience is the family. It is at home that children learn their first lessons in dealing with problems directly rather than letting resentments fester, in noticing the needs of people around them instead of fixating on themselves, of feeling a sense of responsibility toward other people, and in using their time and resources unselfishly. For this reason, a key element for building a just society is to support family life.

Questions for Reflection and Discussion

45 minutes
Choose questions according to your interest and time.

1   What explanation would you offer for the instructions in Leviticus 19:17?

2   In a sentence or two, how would you sum up the impression of holiness that you get from Leviticus 19?

3   Which of the laws in these readings could be enforced by a court? Which couldn't? Why?

4   On the basis of these readings, what kind of person is God?

5   What assumptions do these laws make about what people are like? What assumptions do they make about what people can become?

6   When these laws were written, having a piece of land was a crucial element for living a dignified and constructive life. What elements are necessary today?

7   Who is poor? What is poverty? What other kinds of poverty are there besides lack of money?

8 How can parents raise children who notice and care about others' needs?

9 What experiences of God's mercy motivate you to show mercy to other people? How do you remind yourself of God's mercy to you?

10 What challenges do parents in our society face in raising children with strong moral values, compassion, a sense of social responsibility, and so on? Where can parents find support for their task? How can your parish be helpful?

11 **Focus Question.** In the ancient Near East it was almost impossible for poor people to improve their situation. What factors today tend to keep poor people poor? What could you personally, your parish, your local community, your society do to open more opportunities to poor people to improve their lives?

Prayer to Close

10 minutes
Use this approach—or create your own!

◆ Pray Psalm 146 as praise to
God for the justice and mercy
of his kingdom—and as a
prayer that he would make
his kingdom present for needy
people in our society. End with
an Our Father.

Living Tradition

The Church Responds to Social Changes:
Lending at Interest and Caring for the Environment

This section is a supplement for individual reading.

God spoke his final and complete word to the world when he sent his Son to us as a human being, Jesus of Nazareth. Within a century of Jesus' death, the Spirit finished inspiring the Scriptures that bear witness to him. But that was hardly the end of God's communication with the human race. Century by century, the Spirit has led the Church into a deeper understanding of what God has revealed in Christ and of how to respond to his revelation. In the fourth and fifth centuries, for example, men and women in the monastic movement attained a deeper grasp of the personal dynamics of life in the Spirit, and bishops clarified basic issues about who Jesus is and how he is related to the Father.

Technological, economic, and political changes have also triggered developments in the Church's understanding of the Christian revelation. Ever since the French Revolution in 1789, the leaders of the Church have drawn on Scripture and tradition to show how the Christian revelation illuminates the moral dimension of the social situations that have arisen in the modern age. Modern popes and bishops, especially at Vatican Council II (1962–65), have addressed one subject after another—slavery, labor relations, capitalism, political liberties, abortion, capital punishment—identifying principles expressed in Scripture and showing how they apply to modern situations.

Sometimes in the process, Catholic teaching has seemed to undergo striking changes. This is the case with two of the issues raised by our Scripture readings so far: our responsibility to care for the natural environment and the morality of lending at interest. If you were to compare the current *Catechism of the Catholic Church* (1997) with the previous summary of Catholic teaching, *The Roman Catechism* (1566), you would discover that *The Roman Catechism* contained a section on the immorality of charging interest on loans (section 3:7:11) but said nothing about caring for the environment, while the *Catechism of the Catholic Church* speaks about respect for the environment (sections 2415–2418) but says hardly anything about interest on loans (see section 2269). Yet beneath these changes are basic continuities.

As the current *Catechism of the Catholic Church* points out, Scripture has always taught respect for the natural

39

environment. The current *Catechism* even points out that friendship with animals has been a happy feature of the Catholic tradition. Saints such as St. Francis of Assisi, St. Philip Neri (a dog lover), and, I must mention, St. Kevin were especially fond of animals. But humans' increasing technological dominance of the environment, along with the growth of the biological sciences, has made our responsibility to care for the environment a more pressing issue than it was in 1566. So it is natural for the Church's leaders to say more about it now than they did back then.

Thus the *Catechism of the Catholic Church* teaches: "Use of the mineral, vegetable, and animal resources of the universe cannot be divorced from respect for moral imperatives. Man's dominion over inanimate and other living beings granted by the Creator is not absolute; it is limited by concern for the quality of life of his neighbor, including generations to come; it requires a religious respect for the integrity of creation" (section 2415). *The Catechism* refers to a statement by John Paul II entitled *Centesimus Annus,* or *On the Hundredth Anniversary of Rerum Novarum,* 1991 (sections 37–38). In that statement, the Holy Father wrote (in section 37):

Man, who discovers his capacity to transform and in a certain sense create the world through his own work, forgets that this is always based on God's prior and original gift of the things that are. Man thinks that he can make arbitrary use of the earth, subjecting it without restraint to his will, as though it did not have its own requisites and a prior God-given purpose, which man can indeed develop but must not betray. Instead of carrying out his role as cooperator with God in the work of creation, man sets himself up in place of God and thus ends up provoking a rebellion on the part of nature.

By contrast with environmental responsibility,

the moral issue of lending money at interest has ebbed in modern times. Beginning in the Old Testament period (Leviticus 25:36–37), the biblical and, later, the Christian tradition opposed charging interest on loans. *The Roman Catechism* echoed this tradition when it dealt with taking interest on loans in its section on sins against the seventh commandment—"You shall not steal"

(Exodus 20:15). Charging interest, *The Roman Catechism* said, deserved "special mention—and condemnation" because it involved "exploiting the misery of the poor. . . . Usury, as it is called, is the charging of an amount of money (or its equivalent) to be repaid which is beyond the original amount of money (or its equivalent)." *The Roman Catechism* quoted Jesus against this practice: "Lend, expecting nothing in return" (Luke 6:35).

This condemnation of lending made sense in light of the nature of lending in the past. Before modern commercial and industrial development, lending was not generally a matter of making capital available for business expansion or for major consumer purchases, like buying a house. Lending often involved advancing funds to small farmers to tide them over bad times. Interest on such loans was a profit on others' misery. Demanding that a hungry farmer pay interest on a loan was extortion, a form of theft. This was the basic reason the Church forbade lending at interest.

By the nineteenth century, economic changes were creating new opportunities for borrowers. A person borrowing money to build a factory or a railroad could expect to make large profits from the loan. As profitable new investment opportunities opened up, a lender who did not charge interest on a loan suffered a kind of loss, since he or she could have made some other profitable investment of the money. If a loan was going to enable the borrower to make money, it was only fair that he or she pay interest to compensate the lender for the opportunity to use the funds. In these circumstances, interest on loans has ceased to be extortion and has become a fair way for borrowers to compensate lenders for the use of their funds. Consequently, the Church has removed its strictures against charging interest. The moral principle has not changed: extortion is still wrong. But lending has changed, with the result that taking interest on loans has, generally, ceased to be extortion.

Of course, it is still possible for some lending at interest to constitute extortion. The rates of interest on loans to poor people are sometimes quite high. This may be due in part to a higher risk of default. Nevertheless, the traditional Catholic teaching against charging interest on loans reminds us that high rates of interest on loans to poor people call for moral scrutiny.

Ahab and Jezebel: Power Abusers

Questions to Begin

10 minutes
Use a question or two to get warmed up for the reading.

1   Do you own anything you would never be willing to sell?

2   When is it hard for you to take no for an answer?

This Council lays stress on reverence for man; everyone must consider his every neighbor without exception as another self, taking into account first of all his life and the means necessary to living it with dignity.

The Pope and Bishops of the Catholic Church at Vatican Council II, 1965, *The Church in the Modern World* (section 27)

Opening the Bible

10 minutes
Read the biblical passages aloud. Let individuals take turns
reading paragraphs.

The Background

Last week's readings presented instructions for achieving a just
society. The authors of Scripture, however, were well aware that
people often fail to attain the ideal.

 The Israelites were a rural federation of tribes that had
neither a central government nor a professional standing army.
For various reasons, they suffered repeated military defeats by
the neighboring city-states, which were better organized and
ruled by kings. Many Israelites concluded that they needed a
king of their own to organize and defend them. The central idea
of the Israelites' covenant was that *God* was their king, so God
agreed to their demand for a human king with reluctance—and a
warning that kings would use their position to benefit themselves
and would lead the people back to the same injustices from
which God had rescued them (1 Samuel 4–8).

 The two great early kings of Israel, David and Solomon
(tenth century BC), did indeed treat people as servants (2 Samuel
11–12) and enjoyed an opulent lifestyle (1 Kings 4; 9:15–10:29).
Predictably, their abuse of power alienated many people. The kingdom soon split apart, with the northern tribes seceding and setting
up their own kingdom in the hill country north of Jerusalem (1 Kings
12). The kings of this northern kingdom, called Israel, built a capital
in a place called Samaria. The central character in our reading this
week, Ahab (mid-ninth century BC) is one of these northern kings.

The Reading: 1 Kings 16:29–33; 21:1–24, 27–29

The King Gets What He Wants

16:29 . . . Ahab son of Omri reigned over Israel in Samaria twenty-two
years. 30 Ahab son of Omri did evil in the sight of the LORD more
than all who were before him.

 31 And . . . he took as his wife Jezebel daughter of King Ethbaal
of the Sidonians, and went and served Baal, and worshiped him.
32 He erected an altar for Baal in the house of Baal, which he built

in Samaria. 33 Ahab also made a sacred pole. Ahab did more to provoke the anger of the LORD, the God of Israel, than had all the kings of Israel who were before him.

21:1 Later the following events took place: Naboth the Jezreelite had a vineyard in Jezreel, beside the palace of King Ahab of Samaria. 2 And Ahab said to Naboth, "Give me your vineyard, so that I may have it for a vegetable garden, because it is near my house; I will give you a better vineyard for it; or, if it seems good to you, I will give you its value in money." 3 But Naboth said to Ahab, "The LORD forbid that I should give you my ancestral inheritance."

4 Ahab went home resentful and sullen because of what Naboth the Jezreelite had said to him; for he had said, "I will not give you my ancestral inheritance." He lay down on his bed, turned away his face, and would not eat.

5 His wife Jezebel came to him and said, "Why are you so depressed that you will not eat?" 6 He said to her, "Because I spoke to Naboth the Jezreelite and said to him, 'Give me your vineyard for money; or else, if you prefer, I will give you another vineyard for it'; but he answered, 'I will not give you my vineyard.'" 7 His wife Jezebel said to him, "Do you now govern Israel? Get up, eat some food, and be cheerful; I will give you the vineyard of Naboth the Jezreelite."

8 So she wrote letters in Ahab's name and sealed them with his seal; she sent the letters to the elders and the nobles who lived with Naboth in his city. 9 She wrote in the letters, "Proclaim a fast, and seat Naboth at the head of the assembly; 10 seat two scoundrels opposite him, and have them bring a charge against him, saying, 'You have cursed God and the king.' Then take him out, and stone him to death."

11 The men of his city, the elders and the nobles who lived in his city, did as Jezebel had sent word to them. Just as it was written in the letters that she had sent to them, 12 they proclaimed a fast and seated Naboth at the head of the assembly. 13 The two scoundrels came in and sat opposite him; and the scoundrels brought a charge against Naboth, in the presence of the people, saying, "Naboth cursed God and the king." So they took him outside the city, and stoned him to death. 14 Then they sent to Jezebel, saying, "Naboth has been stoned; he is dead."

15 As soon as Jezebel heard that Naboth had been stoned and was dead, Jezebel said to Ahab, "Go, take possession of the vineyard of

Naboth the Jezreelite, which he refused to give you for money; for Naboth is not alive, but dead." 16 As soon as Ahab heard that Naboth was dead, Ahab set out to go down to the vineyard of Naboth the Jezreelite, to take possession of it.

The King Hears from God

17 Then the word of the LORD came to Elijah the Tishbite, saying: 18 Go down to meet King Ahab of Israel, who rules in Samaria; he is now in the vineyard of Naboth, where he has gone to take possession. 19 You shall say to him, "Thus says the LORD: Have you killed, and also taken possession?" You shall say to him, "Thus says the LORD: In the place where dogs licked up the blood of Naboth, dogs will also lick up your blood."

20 Ahab said to Elijah, "Have you found me, O my enemy?"

He answered, "I have found you. Because you have sold yourself to do what is evil in the sight of the LORD, 21 I will bring disaster on you; I will consume you, and will cut off from Ahab every male, bond or free, in Israel; 22 and I will make your house like the house of Jeroboam son of Nebat, and like the house of Baasha son of Ahijah, because you have provoked me to anger and have caused Israel to sin. 23 Also concerning Jezebel the LORD said, 'The dogs shall eat Jezebel within the bounds of Jezreel.' 24 Anyone belonging to Ahab who dies in the city the dogs shall eat; and anyone of his who dies in the open country the birds of the air shall eat." . . .

27 When Ahab heard those words, he tore his clothes and put sackcloth over his bare flesh; he fasted, lay in the sackcloth, and went about dejectedly. 28 Then the word of the LORD came to Elijah the Tishbite: 29 "Have you seen how Ahab has humbled himself before me? Because he has humbled himself before me, I will not bring the disaster in his days; but in his son's days I will bring the disaster on his house."

First Impression

5 minutes
Briefly mention a question you have about the reading or one thing in it that surprised, impressed, delighted, or challenged you. No discussion! Just listen to one another's reactions.

Exploring the Theme

*If participants have not read this section already, read it aloud.
Otherwise go on to "Questions for Reflection and Discussion."*

B y choosing a king, the Israelites lock themselves into a
conflict. God remains their ultimate king; their covenant with
God continues to provide their basic values and patterns of
life. But the institution of kingship that they have adopted from
their pagan neighbors carries values and practices that conflict
with their covenant with God. Israelite society has been based on
the principle that both people and land belong to God because he
rescued the people from slavery in Egypt and settled them in the
land. But ancient Near Eastern kings regard their lands as their
personal domains and feel free to use their power to increase their
prestige and wealth. God has instructed the Israelites in a way of
life that fosters social justice; it grants special protections to the
poorer and weaker members of society. Under standard Near
Eastern kingship, by contrast, it is accepted that the wealthier and
more powerful people will take advantage of the poorer and
weaker members of society.

1 Kings 16:29–33. Ahab lives in the city of Samaria,
near the present-day Palestinian city of Nablus in the territory
known as the West Bank. He has made an alliance with a
Phoenician king named Ethbaal who rules some cities on the
Mediterranean coast in what is now Lebanon. To cement the
alliance, Ahab marries a daughter of Ethbaal, Jezebel.

As would be expected of a foreign princess, Jezebel brings
her religion with her. Her new husband welcomes her gods. Ahab
sets up a shrine with an altar for Jezebel's chief god and a sacred
pole that symbolizes one of her goddesses. This religious installa-
tion will serve Jezebel and the members of her court who have
accompanied her from Phoenicia, as well as local Canaanite people
in Samaria, who share religious beliefs with the Phoenicians. Ahab
does not abandon the God of Israel, but now he is no longer exclusively loyal to him. While he continues to worship God, he also
worships other gods.

The Phoenician and Canaanite religion in which Jezebel is
steeped is not all bad. It does have morality, social ideals, and a
sense of justice. But the biblical author leaves no doubt that Ahab's
bowing down to Baal is a very bad thing (16:33). One reason is that

the Phoenician and Canaanite deities, unlike the God of Israel, support rulers in using their power for self-aggrandizement. By welcoming Jezebel's gods, Ahab welcomes these values opposed to the Israelite covenant with God. Ahab will find himself caught between two religions, two sets of values, two approaches to the use of political power.

1 Kings 21:1–4. Ahab lives in a fine palace on a pleasant hilltop in Samaria. But he develops an interest in some land next to one of his estates in the nearby Jezreel Valley. He makes a fair offer to the landowner, Naboth, but Naboth is not interested. In Israelite culture, land and family are tied together. Naboth does not want to disrupt his family by selling his land. His "God forbid" (see 21:3) indicates that his refusal has a religious dimension. Naboth takes the view of the land that we saw in Leviticus 25—the land belongs to God. In Naboth's view, God gave a parcel of it to Naboth's ancestors and intends them to keep it. As a tenant on God's land, Naboth has no authority to sell it out of the family. Surely, too, he feels a bond to his particular piece of land because it connects him with his ancestors.

Ahab accepts Naboth's refusal. Or does he? He goes home fuming. Has he given up the idea of getting Naboth's vineyard?

1 Kings 21:5–16. Jezebel grew up in a royal family with a different view of kingship. In her view, Naboth had no right to refuse the king's request to buy his property. Naboth should have recognized a good deal when it was offered to him. Now that he has refused to sell his land to the king, the king is entitled to take action against him. Jezebel knows how her daddy would have handled a problem like Naboth. Relax, she tells her husband. Everything's going to be fine. Her directions to the town elders are ruthless, blunt, and effective. Naboth is killed. His family is thrown off their land.

Ahab loses no time in laying claim to the property. By taking advantage of Jezebel's action, Ahab shares responsibility for it.

1 Kings 21:17–24. Elijah, an Israelite prophet, announces a ferocious divine judgment against Ahab and Jezebel (like verses 23–24, Elijah's words in verses 20–22 are spoken in

God's name). The extreme nature of the punishment indicates God's utter abhorrence at the royal couple's misuse of power, their valuing property above life, their corruption of the judicial system.

1 Kings 21:27–29. Nonetheless, God is willing to forgive. Ahab does not voice his repentance, but his actions express acceptance of God's negative evaluation of his behavior. Hence God removes his judgment; Ahab will avoid punishment. Unfortunately, Ahab does not die peacefully. He stumbles into a self-made disaster by setting out on an unjustified military adventure (1 Kings 22:1–40). Elijah declares that the punishment incurred by Ahab will fall on Ahab's son. It is worth noting that Ahab's son will accumulate enough sins of his own to bring judgment on himself (1 Kings 22:51–53; 2 Kings 1:1–18).

Reflections. Do we, like Ahab, find ourselves caught between two cultures, two sets of values? Much in our political system and popular culture is good. But some secular values conflict with a God-centered view of life: seeking pleasure as a primary goal, exercising freedom without responsibility, counting some people's lives cheaper than others (Do I care how much Malaysian teens got paid for making my running shoes?), wanting more no matter how much we already have. Ahab had a nice palace, but he wasn't satisfied. We, too, live in a culture that encourages us to always want more. Does this lead to justice?

Ahab and Jezebel's abuse of power is food for our thought. We modern readers are not monarchs, but in a democratic society, the people are sovereign. We all share political power. Ahab let something wicked be done in his name and was happy to reap the benefits. Do we allow power to be misused in our name? Would we rather not know some of the things our government does?

The village elders are also thought provoking. Like them, do we face situations (at work? at school?) in which we are pressured to go along with injustice? The elders were not loyal to the ideals of solidarity expressed in our earlier readings. Are we?

45 minutes
Choose questions according to your interest and time.

1 Why would Ahab get so upset at not getting land for a vegetable garden (21:4)? What does his reaction suggest about human beings?

2 Compare what Naboth says to Ahab (21:3) with Ahab's report to Jezebel (21:6). What adjustments in Naboth's statement does Ahab make? Why doesn't he quote Naboth more precisely?

3 What assumptions does Jezebel make in 21:7 about how royal power should be used?

4 In 21:4–6, does Ahab seem to be trying to get Jezebel to deal with Naboth for him?

5 Why do you think the elders carry out Jezebel's instructions (21:11–14)?

6 In 21:16, why doesn't Ahab ask Jezebel what happened to Naboth?

7 How many of the Ten Commandments do Ahab and Jezebel break?

8 How does an individual's relationship with God affect his or her commitment to social justice? What about a society's relationship with God? (Does a modern, democratic society *have* a particular relationship with God?)

9 As consumers, how do we benefit from any unfair arrangements through which our goods and services are supplied? Identify one or two examples of this problem. What responsibilities do consumers have to learn about these problems? What can we do about them?

10 What kinds of injustices should government try to prevent? What kinds should it not try to prevent?

11 **Focus Question.** What responsibility do we, as citizens, bear for the impact of our government's policies on people? What should we do to be informed about what our government does in our name? Offer examples of citizens' involvement in shaping government policies, especially at the level of local government.

Prayer to Close

10 minutes
Use this approach—or create your own!

◆ Take a minute or two to
remember people you know or
have heard about who suffer
some kind of injustice. Then
pray together Psalm 36 or
Psalm 37:1–19 on their behalf.
Take a few minutes for anyone
who wishes to offer a brief
prayer aloud. Close with an
Our Father.

Between Discussions

Human Failures, Divine Promises

Ahab and Elijah illustrate contrary tendencies among the Israelites. Ahab stands for the misuse of power and wealth and the worship of gods who support such behavior. Elijah represents the determination to remain loyal to the God of Israel and to practice justice and compassion. From the ninth to the sixth centuries before Christ, Elijah's approach lost out among the Israelites. Only a minority—prophets and others—stayed faithful to the Israelite covenant and decried the slide away from God and away from social justice.

Kings' abuses of power weakened Israelite society from within. Their unwise foreign policies brought the two small Israelite nations to defeat at the hands of empires based in Mesopotamia (modern Iraq). First to fall was the northern kingdom, Israel (late eighth century BC). Later, the southern kingdom, Judah, also fell (early sixth century BC). Its upper class was taken into exile in Babylon (not far from modern Baghdad).

After a period of soul-searching by the exiles, accompanied by prophecies of restoration by God, the exiles had a chance to return home (mid-sixth century BC). Back in Jerusalem they made a renewed attempt at faithfulness to God and social justice within their community (Nehemiah 5; 9–10). No longer a tribal federation or an independent kingdom, they were now a small community centered on Jerusalem and its temple, in a minor province within the vast Persian Empire (Ezra; Nehemiah).

As we will see in our first reading next week (Isaiah 61:1–9), the restoration of the Israelites (beginning in this period, usually called Jews) was accompanied by prophetic messages announcing that God was beginning to restore justice and peace in the world. The tiny Jewish community in and around Jerusalem fell quite a ways short of this grand prophetic vision. Rather than doubting God's promises, however, Jews concluded that his great act of freedom and judgment lay in the future. Isaiah's prophecy especially was read and pondered by many in the centuries between its delivery and the time of Jesus.

Looking back over the history of Israel, one lesson that emerged with clarity was this: men and women need more divine help in order to be faithful to God and just toward one another. Something *within* people needs to change. Thus, one of the most important promises that God gave through his prophets was that he intended to establish justice in people's hearts. "A new heart I will give you," God assured his people, "and a new spirit I will put within you; and I will remove from your body the heart of stone and give you a heart of flesh. I will put my spirit within you, and make you follow my statutes and be careful to observe my ordinances" (Ezekiel 36:26–27). "I will put my law within them, and I will write it on their hearts; and I will be their God, and they shall be my people" (Jeremiah 31:33). In other prophecies God promised to grant forgiveness and healing (Jeremiah 33:6–11). At the same time, God held out the prospect of liberation to the oppressed and punishment to their oppressors. A descendant of David would lead the charge (Jeremiah 33:14–16).

In our second reading next week, Jesus declares that he has come to fulfill these expectations. Then, in his public ministry, he grants God's forgiveness to sinners. He summons people to a change of heart, especially in their treatment of one another, and especially in their use of material goods and care for the needy. He makes God present; he provides access to God's kingdom. As people sit at table with Jesus, they experience God's kingdom already coming into the world. Around him, among his followers, a new, just society begins to grow. To those who open their hearts to him, he gives the power of divine love, energizing them to live for the good of their neighbors.

Yet Jesus does not strike down oppressors. He does not take power and resources away from those who misuse them. He does not cast the Ahabs and Jezebels of the day from their thrones. God's kingdom is coming through Jesus with the power of love, but not with force and judgment. For now, Jesus establishes social justice by planting new seeds, while leaving the weeds that already fill the field (Matthew 13:24–30).

Jesus' mission is profound and mysterious. As we will see in our third reading, even his close followers have difficulty understanding it.

JESUS: CENTER OF GOD'S PLAN

Questions to Begin

10 minutes
Use a question or two to get warmed up for the reading.

1 When have you been especially glad to go home?

2 When you were a child, did your parents have any habits or customs that you found puzzling? Did they make more sense as you grew older?

The gifts of the Spirit are manifold: some men are called to testify openly to mankind's yearning for its heavenly home and keep the awareness of it vividly before men's minds; others are called to dedicate themselves to the earthly service of men and in this way to prepare the way for the kingdom of heaven.

The Pope and Bishops of the Catholic Church at Vatican Council II, 1965, *The Church in the Modern World* (section 38)

Opening the Bible

10 minutes
Read the biblical passages aloud. Let individuals take turns
reading paragraphs.

The Background

Our three readings concern the coming of God's kingdom. In the first, the prophet Isaiah delivers a message of liberation to Jews in his day, four centuries before Christ. In the second, Jesus reads Isaiah's prophecy aloud and announces to his fellow Jews that the prophecy is now being fulfilled. In the third reading, after Jesus' resurrection his disciples ask him: will God's kingdom now come in fullness?

The Reading: Isaiah 61:1–9; Luke 4:16–30; Acts 1:3–8

A Prophet Announces Release and Renewal

Isaiah 61:1 The spirit of the Lord GOD is upon me,
   because the LORD has anointed me;
he has sent me to bring good news to the oppressed,
   to bind up the brokenhearted,
to proclaim liberty to the captives,
   and release to the prisoners;
2 to proclaim the year of the LORD's favor,
   and the day of vengeance of our God;
   to comfort all who mourn;
3 to provide for those who mourn in Zion—
   to give them a garland instead of ashes,
the oil of gladness instead of mourning,
   the mantle of praise instead of a faint spirit. . . .
4 They shall build up the ancient ruins,
   they shall raise up the former devastations;
they shall repair the ruined cities,
   the devastations of many generations.

5 Strangers shall stand and feed your flocks,
   foreigners shall till your land and dress your vines;
6 but you shall be called priests of the LORD,
   you shall be named ministers of our God;

you shall enjoy the wealth of the nations,
and in their riches you shall glory. . . .

8 For I the LORD love justice,
I hate robbery and wrongdoing;
I will faithfully give them their recompense,
and I will make an everlasting covenant with them.
9 Their descendants shall be known among the nations,
and their offspring among the peoples;
all who see them shall acknowledge
that they are a people whom the LORD has blessed.

Now the Prophecy Will Be Fulfilled

Luke 4:16 When he came to Nazareth, where he had been brought up, he went to the synagogue on the sabbath day, as was his custom. He stood up to read, 17 and the scroll of the prophet Isaiah was given to him. He unrolled the scroll and found the place where it was written:
18 "The Spirit of the Lord is upon me,
because he has anointed me
to bring good news to the poor.
He has sent me to proclaim release to the captives
and recovery of sight to the blind,
to let the oppressed go free,
19 to proclaim the year of the Lord's favor."

20 And he rolled up the scroll, gave it back to the attendant, and sat down. The eyes of all in the synagogue were fixed on him. 21 Then he began to say to them, "Today this scripture has been fulfilled in your hearing."

22 All spoke well of him and were amazed at the gracious words that came from his mouth. They said, "Is not this Joseph's son?"

23 He said to them, "Doubtless you will quote to me this proverb, 'Doctor, cure yourself!' And you will say, 'Do here also in your hometown the things that we have heard you did at Capernaum.'"
24 And he said, "Truly I tell you, no prophet is accepted in the prophet's hometown. 25 But the truth is, there were many widows in Israel in the time of Elijah, when the heaven was shut up three years and six months, and there was a severe famine over all the land; 26 yet Elijah was sent to none of them except to a widow at Zarephath in Sidon.

27 There were also many lepers in Israel in the time of the prophet Elisha, and none of them was cleansed except Naaman the Syrian."

28 When they heard this, all in the synagogue were filled with rage. 29 They got up, drove him out of the town, and led him to the brow of the hill on which their town was built, so that they might hurl him off the cliff. 30 But he passed through the midst of them and went on his way.

A Question about God's Kingdom

Acts 1:3 After his suffering he presented himself alive to them by many convincing proofs, appearing to them during forty days and speaking about the kingdom of God. 4 While staying with them, he ordered them not to leave Jerusalem, but to wait there for the promise of the Father. "This," he said, "is what you have heard from me; 5 for John baptized with water, but you will be baptized with the Holy Spirit not many days from now."

6 So when they had come together, they asked him, "Lord, is this the time when you will restore the kingdom to Israel?"

7 He replied, "It is not for you to know the times or periods that the Father has set by his own authority. 8 But you will receive power when the Holy Spirit has come upon you; and you will be my witnesses in Jerusalem, in all Judea and Samaria, and to the ends of the earth."

First Impression

5 minutes
Briefly mention a question you have about the reading or one thing in it that surprised, impressed, delighted, or challenged you. No discussion! Just listen to one another's reactions.

Exploring the Theme

If participants have not read this section already, read it aloud. Otherwise go on to "Questions for Reflection and Discussion."

Since you've done your homework by reading Leviticus 25 (Week 2), you can recognize Isaiah's prophecy for what it is: the announcement of a jubilee year.

Isaiah 61:1–9. Isaiah declares "liberty" (61:1)—the same Hebrew word was used in Leviticus 25:10. By order of the divine king, Isaiah announces, debts are hereby forgiven; debtors are released from slavery. Earlier prophecies in the book of Isaiah announced that God was going to free the Israelites exiled in Mesopotamia and allow them to return to their homeland. Isaiah's message in our reading this week (61:2–3) picks up this message of comfort and joy and applies it to the next generation of Jews. The exiles who have returned to Jerusalem are facing economic and political problems. Isaiah announces that God is continuing to act on their behalf. The exiles may not yet experience it, but God has indeed already acted to liberate them from their difficulties. As a comparison, picture a U.S. military officer riding up to a plantation in Alabama in 1865, calling the slaves together, and announcing that the Confederate government has collapsed. Since the Emancipation Proclamation has now come into effect in Alabama, he tells them, "You're free. You can go now."

Isaiah speaks of "the day of vengeance of our God" (61:2). The translation is somewhat misleading. Angry human individuals take vengeance, but God feels no bitterness, no desire to inflict pain. God establishes justice. The day of God's "vengeance" will be the moment when he exercises his supreme judicial authority over the human race and puts an end to all wrongdoing, when he abolishes everything that interferes with social justice. Although God is not vengeful, his judgment will be painful for oppressors, since he will take away their power. Again, as a comparison, recall that freeing the slaves in the American South involved defeating the Confederate army.

Isaiah does not use the term "kingdom of God." But his message expresses the idea that God is the king of the earth and is now using his authority to help the poor and oppressed Jews. There *is* going to be social justice! Yet, while Jerusalem was rebuilt, the restoration was limited. The day of the Lord's judgment did not come. Many Jewish people concluded that Isaiah's prophecy must refer to a liberation and judgment by God at some future time.

Luke 4:14–30. Early in his ministry, Jesus visits Nazareth, where he grew up. On the Sabbath he goes to the synagogue to join in the community's prayer. Perhaps before the service he asks the synagogue official for permission to do the reading, for after the opening prayers the official hands the scroll of Isaiah to him. Unrolling it, Jesus reads aloud the same prophetic announcement we have just read. Then he makes an electrifying declaration: this prophecy is now being fulfilled!

The Galilean peasants in the little synagogue are pleased by Jesus' declaration. What do they think he means? They are poor, oppressed by unscrupulous rulers, absentee landlords, loan sharks, and corrupt tax collectors. Quite possibly they think Jesus is announcing that God is about to cure their economic ills and liberate them from their oppressors.

The people of Nazareth seem eager to see Jesus work some miraculous healings in his hometown (4:23). But he refuses. In explanation, he compares his ministry to that of two Old Testament prophets, Elijah and Elisha. Referring to incidents in those prophets' lives (1 Kings 17:9; 2 Kings 5:1–19), Jesus makes it clear that in his ministry God is going to act on behalf of captive and oppressed people outside of Israel as well as within. In effect, he informs his former townspeople that their membership in the people of Israel does not give them any special claim to God's liberating action.

Notice that Jesus is silent on the issue of God's bringing judgment on those who cause injustice. Isaiah seemed to suggest that God was going to humble the enemies of the people of Israel (Isaiah 61:5–6), but Jesus does not quote this part of Isaiah's prophecy. Rather, Jesus cuts off his quotation from Isaiah before the part about God's "vengeance" (Isaiah 61:2). If the people of Nazareth have been hoping that the moment has arrived for God to bring judgment and destruction on those who are responsible for social injustices, they are going to be disappointed.

59

Yet Jesus has declared that the prophecy of Isaiah *is being fulfilled* as he speaks. Like Isaiah—indeed, even more than Isaiah—Jesus proclaims that God's act of liberating the oppressed and establishing social justice *has begun.* As Jesus stands preaching in the synagogue of Nazareth, the great jubilee has arrived. Debts are released; slaves are free to return home. What does he mean?

During his earthly life, Jesus has come not to bring judgment on those who are responsible for injustices but to call men and women to repentance and to grant them forgiveness. Jesus picks up the preaching of John the Baptist, who proclaimed "repentance for the forgiveness of sins" (Luke 3:3). When Jesus announces God's release of debts and liberation of slaves in the Nazareth synagogue, he means release from the debts and slavery of sin (he speaks of sins as debts in Luke 11:4). Release from our sins enables us, like debt slaves freed from bondage, to begin to make our way home—not to a piece of ancestral land but to our true and eternal home in God's kingdom (Luke 23:43).

But what *event* does Jesus announce? What action has God taken to bring release and freedom from sins? God's action is, first, the coming of his Son. God's forgiveness and his reign over men and women have now become present in Jesus (Luke 5:24). This is the message of Jesus' miracles of healing and feeding and raising the dead: they signal that God's kingdom is present *in him.* Men and women who follow Jesus will experience the liberating power of God's kingdom, first of all in their own hearts and lives. Through his presence and example (see Matthew 11:29) they will grow into men and women who contribute to social justice by the way they live. Soon there will be a second stage to God's act of liberation: Jesus will accept suffering and death and will rise from death to glory. Through this, God will make his forgiveness and life available to men and women everywhere (Luke 24:44–47).

But what about the liberation from all forms of evil in human society and the final establishment of justice that Isaiah announced? When will that be? This is the question that Jesus' disciples put to him in our third reading.

4

Acts 1:3–8. Jesus' disciples have had a hard time understanding his plans. First, there was the profound difficulty of grasping that he was going to bring God's reign by dying on a cross (Luke 24:25–27). Even now, after he has died and risen from the dead, they do not understand how God's kingdom is coming through him. They expect him to quickly fulfill the promise of liberation and justice in Isaiah's prophecy. *Now,* they think, God will show his special favor to the people of Israel and overthrow all the forces that prevent them from enjoying justice and peace. Now God will now restore independence to Israel, establish a just regime, and repel oppressors. Probably the disciples would like to see some divine "vengeance" directed against the Romans.

While Jesus has inaugurated God's kingdom in the world, however, he indicates that some time will elapse before the kingdom fully arrives. For the present, he gives his followers an important assignment. They are to proclaim the jubilee year that has now begun. This means alerting people to the coming of God's kingdom through Jesus' death and resurrection and inviting them to experience God's forgiveness through a personal relationship with the risen Lord. Jesus' disciples are to be his "witnesses"—to tell people what they know about him from their personal experience. The Spirit will enable them to do it.

Apparently, the disciples were hoping for a more immediate completion of God's kingdom, with a more forceful establishment of justice in the world. But when Jesus makes his final departure and the Spirit comes to them, they will see results that will perhaps surprise them (more on this in Week 6).

Reflections. The one who will ultimately bring justice and peace to the human race is already among us: Jesus Christ! In the end, Jesus will disarm all evil powers; he will liberate all the oppressed. Already, by his death and resurrection, he gives us access to God's forgiveness. He extends an invitation to all of us to repent, to change, to become involved in what he is doing in the world. Many questions remain, but this week's readings give us a great deal to be glad about.

Questions for Reflection and Discussion

45 minutes
Choose questions according to your interest and time.

1   Why might the people in Nazareth wish to see Jesus' miracle-working power (Luke 4:23)?

2   Why were the people of Nazareth so angry at Jesus (Luke 4:28–29)?

3   Many of the people who listened to Jesus preach the coming of God's kingdom were hoping that God would bring justice to society. How did his program for dealing with the sufferings caused by injustices in society differ from their expectations?

4   In what ways are sins like debts—to God or to other people? What are consequences of the indebtedness of sin? In what ways do forgiveness by God and by other people bring release and freedom? Illustrate your answers from your own experiences or from situations you have witnessed.

5   What part does forgiveness play in creating a just society?

6 When have you had to struggle to understand God and how he acts in people's lives? What did you learn?

7 What is Jesus inviting you to do in response to his commission in Acts 1:8?

8 **Focus Question.** Isaiah (61:1–2) and Jesus (Luke 4:18–19) announce that God is bringing freedom and "release." In our society, who would welcome freedom and release? Pick one or two situations and consider how you and others could be instruments of freedom and release for them. What kinds of indebtedness are within your personal power to release? What action could you take?

Prayer to Close

10 minutes
Use this approach—or create your own!

◆ Pray the prayer of our Lady in which she celebrates the coming of God's kingdom through her Son (Luke 1:46–55). Notice what she says about the benefits his coming will bring for all who are deprived of justice or lack the necessities of life. Pause for participants to offer aloud any brief prayers they may wish. Close with a Hail Mary.

Living Tradition

Take the Pledge

This section is a supplement for individual reading.

Pope John Paul II declared the year 2000 a jubilee year for the Church. He encouraged Christians to celebrate this jubilee by seeking and granting forgiveness and renewing their commitment to bring freedom and support to those in need. To help Catholics respond to the pope's appeal, the bishops in the United States composed a statement of commitment for individuals and groups. While the 2000 jubilee year has passed, the pope's appeal and the bishops' statement remain valid, because the jubilee that Jesus proclaimed in the synagogue of Nazareth (Luke 4:16–21) continues today.

Jubilee Pledge for Charity, Justice, and Peace
A Catholic Commitment for the New Millennium

The jubilee of our Lord's birth calls us "to bring glad tidings to the poor. . . . to proclaim liberty to captives and recovery of sight to the blind, to let the oppressed go free" (Luke 4:18).

As disciples of Jesus in the new millennium, I/we pledge to:
Pray regularly for greater justice and peace.
Learn more about Catholic social teaching and its call to protect human life, stand with the poor, and care for creation.
Reach across boundaries of religion, race, ethnicity, gender, and disabling conditions.
Live justly in family life, school, work, the marketplace, and the political arena.
Serve those who are poor and vulnerable, sharing more time and talent.
Give more generously to those in need at home and abroad.
Advocate for public policies that protect human life, promote human dignity, preserve God's creation, and build peace.
Encourage others to work for greater charity, justice, and peace.

_____

Signature

From *Everyday Christianity: To Hunger and Thirst for Justice. A Pastoral Reflection on Lay Discipleship for Justice in a New Millennium.*

DISCIPLES: THOSE WHO SERVE

Questions to Begin

10 minutes
Use a question or two to get warmed up for the reading.

1 When was the last time you declined an invitation?

2 How close have you ever gotten to a camel?

We have been warned . . . that it profits man nothing if he gains the whole world and loses or forfeits himself. Far from diminishing our concern to develop this earth, the expectancy of a new earth should spur us on, for it is here that the body of a new human family grows, foreshadowing in some way the age which is to come.

The Pope and Bishops of the Catholic Church at Vatican Council II, 1965, *The Church in the Modern World* (section 39)

10 minutes
Read the biblical passages aloud. Let individuals take turns reading paragraphs.

The Background

Our last reading left the disciples—and us—in a state of hope, but with many questions. In Jesus, God has made his central move for bringing the human race back into a close relationship with himself and leading us toward a just life with one another. But now that Jesus has died and risen, how does God's plan work out in the world? The answers began to emerge in the events that followed Jesus' final departure from his disciples at his ascension, when the Holy Spirit came to them. These events will be the subject of our readings next week. But before we go forward to those events, we need to go back to Jesus' earthly ministry.

While it is important to gain some insight into God's plans for the world, it is also crucial to grasp how his plans play out on the personal level. God's plans for the world move forward through individual men and women—through us. Our readings this week spotlight issues each of us faces as we seek to find our place in God's plans. Jesus calls his disciples to be personally with him, to have a change of heart, to imitate him. As we live in this relationship of discipleship with Jesus, we are changed. We become people who can better shoulder our responsibilities for justice in the various spheres of our lives.

Our readings this week capture moments in Jesus' ministry as he is on his way to Jerusalem to die. He calls his followers to follow him not just in the literal sense of walking with him to Jerusalem but in the sense of joining him in the work that he is about in the world. He is on his way to relinquish his life on behalf of others. His conversations reveal what this means for his disciples.

The Reading: Mark 8:31–35; 10:42–45; 10:17–30

Jesus Challenges His Disciples . . .

8:31 Then he began to teach them that the Son of Man must undergo great suffering, and be rejected by the elders, the chief priests, and the scribes, and be killed, and after three days rise again. 32 He said all this quite openly. And Peter took him aside and began to rebuke him. [33] But turning and looking at his disciples, he rebuked Peter and said, "Get behind me, Satan! For you are setting your mind not on divine things but on human things."

[34] He called the crowd with his disciples, and said to them, "If any want to become my followers, let them deny themselves and take up their cross and follow me. [35] For those who want to save their life will lose it, and those who lose their life for my sake, and for the sake of the gospel, will save it."

. . . And Sets an Example

[10:42] . . . Jesus called them and said to them, "You know that among the Gentiles those whom they recognize as their rulers lord it over them, and their great ones are tyrants over them. [43] But it is not so among you; but whoever wishes to become great among you must be your servant, [44] and whoever wishes to be first among you must be slave of all. [45] For the Son of Man came not to be served but to serve, and to give his life a ransom for many."

An Invitation to Discipleship

[10:17] As he was setting out on a journey, a man ran up and knelt before him, and asked him, "Good Teacher, what must I do to inherit eternal life?"

[18] Jesus said to him, "Why do you call me good? No one is good but God alone. [19] You know the commandments: 'You shall not murder; You shall not commit adultery; You shall not steal; You shall not bear false witness; You shall not defraud; Honor your father and mother.'"

[20] He said to him, "Teacher, I have kept all these since my youth."

[21] Jesus, looking at him, loved him and said, "You lack one thing; go, sell what you own, and give the money to the poor, and you will have treasure in heaven; then come, follow me."

[22] When he heard this, he was shocked and went away grieving, for he had many possessions.

[23] Then Jesus looked around and said to his disciples, "How hard it will be for those who have wealth to enter the kingdom of

God!" 24 And the disciples were perplexed at these words. But Jesus said to them again, "Children, how hard it is to enter the kingdom of God! 25 It is easier for a camel to go through the eye of a needle than for someone who is rich to enter the kingdom of God."

26 They were greatly astounded and said to one another, "Then who can be saved?"

27 Jesus looked at them and said, "For mortals it is impossible, but not for God; for God all things are possible."

28 Peter began to say to him, "Look, we have left everything and followed you."

29 Jesus said, "Truly I tell you, there is no one who has left house or brothers or sisters or mother or father or children or fields, for my sake and for the sake of the good news, 30 who will not receive a hundredfold now in this age—houses, brothers and sisters, mothers and children, and fields with persecutions—and in the age to come eternal life."

First Impression

5 minutes
Briefly mention a question you have about the reading or one thing in it that surprised, impressed, delighted, or challenged you. No discussion! Just listen to one another's reactions.

Exploring the Theme

If participants have not read this section already, read it aloud. Otherwise go on to "Questions for Reflection and Discussion."

Mark 8:34–35; 10:42–45. Jesus sets two ways of living before us. We can seek to save our lives in this world and to get others to serve our needs. Or we can invest our lives in him, seek the life to come in God's kingdom, and devote ourselves to serving other people. As human beings, we typically try to advance our own interests. Jesus proposes we use our abilities and resources for others. Jesus is a man turned outward toward other people. He invites us to become like him.

Jesus sets forth an ideal of service. The Greek word for "servant" in 10:43 (the related word for "serve" is used in 10:45) does not imply anything menial. It refers to carrying out the wishes of someone else, providing what someone else needs, acting as a go-between for others. The word can be applied to an ambassador representing a government or to a waiter serving guests in a restaurant. Thus Jesus is not recommending that his followers take the lowliest jobs. A person does not serve more by mopping the company's restrooms than by sitting at the president's desk. One serves by focusing on others' needs rather than on one's own, whatever one's job may be.

Money and possessions are areas where we face decisions about whether and how to serve. So it is not surprising that Jesus deals with this subject in several episodes in the Gospels. Our next reading is one of them.

Mark 10:17–30. A man asks Jesus how to enter eternal life (10:17), that is, the kingdom of God, the age to come (10:30). Jesus responds with something familiar to the man: keep the Ten Commandments. Possibly because the man looks like a wealthy landowner, Jesus adds, "You shall not defraud" (10:19), which would mean, Do not exploit your fieldworkers.

The man declares that he has kept these commandments, and Jesus seems to accept his self-evaluation. But does the man keep the *first* commandment: does he love God? Jesus has reminded the man that God alone is good (10:18). Is God the great good toward which this man is directing his life? To bring the answer to light, Jesus makes an astonishing invitation. "Sell everything you own. Give the proceeds to your needy neighbors. Then become my follower."

The invitation forces the man to look into his heart and ask himself what he values most. If he finds that he is divided between love of God and love of self, Jesus' offer of discipleship offers the means to overcome his inner conflict. Jesus' love for the man ("Jesus, looking at him, loved him"—10:21) will sustain him in the process of growing to love God single-heartedly.

The man looks into his heart. What he sees is his love for his possessions. For him, God is not fully God. But, he decides, that is how it will be. Jesus has offered him the opportunity to gain the "one thing" he lacks (10:21)—a heart set on God—but he turns down the invitation. His love of riches (4:19) strangles God's word to him. By declining Jesus' offer of discipleship, the man declines to get on the road to God's kingdom. Thus Jesus' sad comment as the man walks away: "See how hard it is for a rich person to enter God's kingdom! Why," Jesus remarks, "it's impossible!" (See 10:25.)

Jesus goes on to say that God can do what people cannot (10:27). Does he mean that God will bring us into his kingdom even though we love money? Nowhere does Jesus ever suggest that if we reject his words and refuse to follow him we will enter eternal life anyway. As we have seen, Jesus warns us of what will happen if we choose self rather than God, if we serve ourselves rather than our neighbors, if we save our lives in this world rather than losing them to gain life in the kingdom to come (8:34–35). Here, then, Jesus seems to mean that God can enable us to do what we cannot do by ourselves: God can empower us to serve our neighbors, to let go of our lives in this world so as to gain our lives in the world to come. Jesus' disciples reflect the effectiveness of this divine help. They have begun to do what Jesus invited the wealthy man to do. They have left all to follow Jesus (10:28).

Jesus' call to the man is unusually demanding. Leaving everything behind is necessary for anyone traveling with Jesus from town to town. But Jesus has not required all those who believe in him to travel with him (consider Mary and Martha—Luke 10:38–42; John 11; 12:1-8).

And even those who join Jesus in his travels do not necessarily *sell* everything they own. Peter has left home (10:28), but still seems to have his house in Capernaum, since he uses it when he is in town (Mark 2:1, compare 1:29; Matthew 17:24–27). Thus Jesus' reason for wanting this man to sell his possessions cannot be simply that he wants him to be free to accompany him on his travels. Jesus' radical requirement seems to be specially tailored for this man. What is it about him that makes the requirement appropriate? The only particular thing about the man that Mark tells us is his wealth. Perhaps his wealth is the reason Jesus gives him such a radical call: being wealthy, he is strongly attached to his possessions and so needs to break with them decisively.

Notice that Jesus makes a further specification. The man is to sell his property *and give the proceeds to the poor.* Rather than turning his possessions over to his family, Jesus wants him to use his property to care for his needy neighbors. Jesus underlines the importance of this action by assuring the man that it will bring him "treasure in heaven" (10:21). Thus it is part of the answer to the man's original question (10:17). Jesus has come to serve; he devotes himself to the well-being of his fellow human beings (10:42–45). He invites his followers to share in his ministry. Since this man's ample resources enable him to share in Jesus' ministry in a material way, that is what Jesus expects him to do.

Jesus does not imply there is anything wrong with the man's wealth. His wealth is not to be destroyed but distributed. It is not a curse but a blessing. The man would prefer to keep this blessing for himself and add a heavenly blessing to it. But Jesus advises him to pass the blessing on to others. He wants the man to reorient himself away from seeking his own good and toward seeking what is good for his neighbors.

Finally, Jesus speaks about the community that is growing up around him. Some disciples leave home; other disciples stay in their homes and make them available to those who travel (10:30—the houses that the traveling disciples will receive a hundredfold are those of brothers and sisters in the Christian movement who stay at home). But all the members of the community forsake all in the sense of devoting themselves fully to the service of others.

The disciples have left all, but they have not yet arrived in the kingdom. Their attitudes still need a lot of adjustment, as the next episode demonstrates (10:35–41). But they are on the way. They are experiencing the blessing of Jesus' presence, as well as the blessings of each other (10:30). The rich man walked away from this. He focused on what he would lose by following Jesus, rather than on what he would gain.

Reflections. Whether or not we are called to leave home, family, and normal employment in order to follow Jesus, being his disciples means leaving all in the sense of making his will our highest priority. Living for life in "the age to come" rather than for life in "this age" (10:30), seeking to serve others rather than ourselves—this lifestyle is for all of us, and it has implications for how we handle our money, resources, talents, and so on.

Leaving all to follow Jesus is not a once-and-for-all decision. The question of who and what we love is never finally settled in this life. We constantly face new opportunities to put ourselves and our resources at the service of those in need. For the man in the story, giving away and leaving behind was a necessary first step in following Jesus. For us, it is necessary to continue to give away and continue to leave behind in order to keep following Jesus on the path he has marked out for us.

Discipleship to Jesus is at the heart of living for social justice. Jesus calls us, like the rich man, to reject the idolatry of money, to stop worshiping the comfort, security, and prestige that money brings. Only as we get free from this idolatry—by God's grace (10:27)—can we play our role in building society according to God's purposes. The saints demonstrate that those who make the most radical response to Jesus' call become especially industrious and effective in contributing to justice in the world.

Questions for Reflection and Discussion

45 minutes
Choose questions according to your interest and time.

1 Jesus says that the person who follows him must "deny" himself or herself (Mark 8:34). What does he mean by this?

2 Jesus speaks of losing one's life for his sake and of serving other people (8:35 and 10:43). What's the connection?

3 What is Jesus' idea of greatness (Mark 10:43)?

4 Jesus summons each of his disciples to become a "slave of all" (10:44). What does he mean? What examples might illustrate what Jesus does and does not mean?

5 Besides money and property, what other kinds of wealth do people have?

6 Jesus advises the rich man to give away his property to those who are in material need. What other sorts of need do people experience? What sorts of things does Jesus invite us to give away to help meet these nonmaterial needs?

7 When have you let go of something in order to be free to follow Jesus and be of service to other people? What was the outcome of your decision? How could you apply what you learned to a situation in your life today?

8 Identify a situation in which people experience injustice or need. Suggest how the approach to life that Jesus speaks about in Mark 8 and 10 might lead a person to try to improve the situation.

9 For personal reflection: What do I have? What do I love? What hold do my money and possessions have on me? Do I recognize God as the one good? Do I love him with all my strength and resources?

10 Focus Question. How is Jesus calling you to use your time and material resources for the good of others? What is he inviting you to give up in order to be available to serve your family, friends, people at your workplace, in your community?

Prayer to Close

10 minutes
Use this approach—or create your own!

◆ Ask one participant to read
Mark 10:17–22 aloud again.
Pause for silent reflection. Then
pray this prayer together. Close
with an Our Father.

Lord, thank you for all your gifts
to us. Lead us to love you, the
giver, more than the gifts you
give. Teach us to be as generous
with others as you have been
with us. Guide us in using your
gifts to serve your purposes. Help
us to put aside everything else to
follow you.

Saints in the Making
A Midlife Call to Serve

This section is a supplement for individual reading.

G o, sell what you own, and give the money to the poor . . . ; then come, follow me" (Mark 10:21). From the neatness of Jesus' proposal to the rich man, it almost seems as though Jesus was planning to stand and wait while the man went, sold, distributed, and returned to join the group of disciples—all between lunch and dinner. Often, however, the leaving-giving-and-following is a messy and lengthy process.

Rose Hawthorne Lathrop began life in privileged, if not wealthy, circumstances in 1851. Her father was the well-known author Nathaniel Hawthorne. Rose received a refined education in Massachusetts, England, and Germany. While she was growing up, prominent intellectuals visited in her home. Her aunts were leaders in the development of the public school system in the United States. At twenty, she married her teen sweetheart, George Lathrop, a talented young writer. She had literary ambitions of her own.

One by one, Rose's hopes were disappointed. Her writing found little public acceptance. Her only child died at the age of four. Her husband developed a drinking problem. Rose had grown up in a religiously earnest home. Over the years she—and George—made a serious search for God. After twenty years of marriage, they entered the Catholic Church together. Nevertheless, in 1895, she separated from him. It might have seemed that Rose's life was over. As it turned out, it was about to begin anew.

In 1896, Rose was in New York City and visited a friend who was dying of cancer in a municipal institution on Blackwell's Island (today called Roosevelt Island). The misery Rose saw at Blackwell's Island appalled her. "A fire was then lighted in my heart," she wrote later, "where it still burns. I set my whole being to endeavor to bring consolation to the cancerous poor." And that is exactly what she did, until her death thirty years later.

Beginning with visiting impoverished cancer victims in their homes and taking them into her own apartment, Rose drew together women dedicated to caring for terminal cancer patients who lacked financial resources. Rose and her helpers became a religious order, the Dominican Sisters of Hawthorne. Today they operate six residential nursing facilities in five states.

Between Discussions

Who Is My Neighbor?

The Gospels tell us of another man who asked Jesus the question posed by the rich man in our last reading. The conversation between this second man, who is a lawyer, and Jesus is fundamental for understanding Jesus' approach to social justice. Here is the episode, with a few comments.

Luke 10:25 . . . A lawyer stood up to test Jesus. "Teacher," he said, "what must I do to inherit eternal life?"

26 He said to him, "What is written in the law? What do you read there?"

27 He answered, "You shall love the Lord your God with all your heart, and with all your soul, and with all your strength, and with all your mind; and your neighbor as yourself."

28 And he said to him, "You have given the right answer; do this, and you will live."

29 But wanting to justify himself, he asked Jesus, "And who is my neighbor?"

30 Jesus replied, "A man was going down from Jerusalem to Jericho, and fell into the hands of robbers, who stripped him, beat him, and went away, leaving him half dead. 31 Now by chance a priest was going down that road; and when he saw him, he passed by on the other side. 32 So likewise a Levite, when he came to the place and saw him, passed by on the other side. 33 But a Samaritan while traveling came near him; and when he saw him, he was moved with pity. 34 He went to him and bandaged his wounds, having poured oil and wine on them. Then he put him on his own animal, brought him to an inn, and took care of him. 35 The next day he took out two denarii, gave them to the innkeeper, and said, 'Take care of him; and when I come back, I will repay you whatever more you spend.' 36 Which of these three, do you think, was a neighbor to the man who fell into the hands of the robbers?"

37 He said, "The one who showed him mercy."

Jesus said to him, "Go and do likewise."

Perhaps because this man is trained in the Mosaic law, Jesus invites him to answer his own question. The man combines passages from Scripture to express a two-part command: love God and neighbor. Jesus expresses approval. This is the path to eternal life.

The "love your neighbor" part is familiar to us from our readings in Week 2, where we met it in its original context— Leviticus 19. There "neighbor" is a fellow Israelite. So the lawyer's question is a good one. Are only Jews (only good Jews?) my neighbors?

In Jesus' story, a Jewish man is injured, but two fellow Jews—given their jobs, they are as Jewish as anyone could be— ignore his plight. A foreigner, however, goes out of his way to help the man.

Innkeepers were not generally considered an especially honest group, yet the Samaritan traveler trusts this innkeeper to use his money to care for the injured man. The innkeeper, in turn, trusts the Samaritan to come back and cover any further expenses. The two men seem to know each other. Perhaps the Samaritan is a regular first-century road warrior on the Jerusalem– Jericho route. Are the oil and wine he carries marketing samples? In any case, he and the innkeeper make a happy contrast to the other pair—the coldhearted priest and Levite. The Samaritan and the innkeeper come from the sometimes shady world of first- century business travel, yet they have more common decency than the priest and the Levite, whose world is the temple.

Jesus tells the lawyer to do what the Samaritan did. What the Samaritan did is this: he did not ask the lawyer's question. When he saw someone in need, he did not stop to wonder whether that person was his neighbor. He already knew.

For all their long hours of offerings and prayers in the temple, the priest and the Levite feel nothing toward the injured man—except perhaps disgust or fear. What sets the Samaritan apart is simply that he feels compassion (10:33). This is not a special refinement acquired only after much training. It is the ordinary human response to a fellow human being in pain. The priest and Levite do not have this minimum level of fellow feeling. Their religious involvement seems to have made them not more human but less. The lesson—and warning—for ourselves is plain enough.

THE CHURCH: YEAST IN THE DOUGH

Questions to Begin

10 minutes
Use a question or two to get warmed up for the reading.

1 What's the most encouraging thing anyone ever said to you?

2 If you could hand off some regular task to someone else, what would it be?

After we have obeyed the Lord, and in His Spirit nurtured on earth the values of human dignity, brotherhood and freedom, and indeed all the good fruits of our nature and enterprise, we will find them again, but freed of stain, burnished and transfigured. This will be so when Christ hands over to the Father a kingdom eternal and universal: "a kingdom of truth and life, of holiness and grace, of justice, love, and peace."

The Pope and Bishops of the Catholic Church at Vatican Council II, 1965, *The Church in the Modern World* (section 39)

Opening the Bible

10 minutes
Read the biblical passages aloud. Let individuals take turns reading paragraphs.

The Background

Earlier we read an excerpt from the beginning of Luke's Acts of the Apostles (1:3–8, Week 4). The disciples asked Jesus to explain the timing of the coming of God's kingdom. Jesus gave them only a brief answer that pointed them toward the coming of the Holy Spirit and their task of evangelization. Now we return to Acts to see how the disciples learned more of the answer to their question. Not that the Spirit gave them more precise information about the final coming of God's kingdom. He did not. But as the Spirit empowered the disciples to bear witness to Jesus, they saw God's kingdom coming in a less overt but nevertheless powerful way. People coming to faith in Jesus were drawn into a common life centered on him. Within this community, signs of God's restoration of social justice in the world quickly appeared.

Our readings from Acts take up the story after Jesus' departure from his disciples by his ascension to heaven. As our first reading begins, the Holy Spirit has just come to the disciples, and Peter, their representative, has given his first sermon explaining who Jesus is and what role he has played in God's plans for the world.

The Reading: Acts 2:41–47; 4:32–37; 6:1–7; 9:36–42; 11:27–30; Matthew 13:33

The Christian Community Springs to Life

Acts 2:41 . . . Those who welcomed his message were baptized, and that day about three thousand persons were added. 42 They devoted themselves to the apostles' teaching and fellowship, to the breaking of bread and the prayers.

43 Awe came upon everyone, because many wonders and signs were being done by the apostles. 44 All who believed were together and had all things in common; 45 they would sell their possessions and goods and distribute the proceeds to all, as any had need. 46 Day by day, as they spent much time together in the temple, they broke bread at home and ate their food with glad and generous hearts,

⁴⁷ praising God and having the goodwill of all the people. And day by day the Lord added to their number those who were being saved.

Bearing Witness, Meeting Needs

Acts 4:32 Now the whole group of those who believed were of one heart and soul, and no one claimed private ownership of any possessions, but everything they owned was held in common. ³³ With great power the apostles gave their testimony to the resurrection of the Lord Jesus, and great grace was upon them all. ³⁴ There was not a needy person among them, for as many as owned lands or houses sold them and brought the proceeds of what was sold. ³⁵ They laid it at the apostles' feet, and it was distributed to each as any had need.

³⁶ There was a Levite, a native of Cyprus, Joseph, to whom the apostles gave the name Barnabas (which means "son of encouragement"). ³⁷ He sold a field that belonged to him, then brought the money, and laid it at the apostles' feet.

Growing Pains

Acts 6:1 Now during those days, when the disciples were increasing in number, the Hellenists complained against the Hebrews because their widows were being neglected in the daily distribution of food. ² And the twelve called together the whole community of the disciples and said, "It is not right that we should neglect the word of God in order to wait on tables. ³ Therefore, friends, select from among yourselves seven men of good standing, full of the Spirit and of wisdom, whom we may appoint to this task, ⁴ while we, for our part, will devote ourselves to prayer and to serving the word."

⁵ What they said pleased the whole community, and they chose Stephen, a man full of faith and the Holy Spirit, together with Philip, Prochorus, Nicanor, Timon, Parmenas, and Nicolaus, a proselyte of Antioch. ⁶ They had these men stand before the apostles, who prayed and laid their hands on them.

⁷ The word of God continued to spread; the number of the disciples increased greatly in Jerusalem, and a great many of the priests became obedient to the faith.

A Remarkable Woman Is Remarkably Revived

Acts 9:36 Now in Joppa there was a disciple whose name was Tabitha, which in Greek is Dorcas. She was devoted to good works and acts of charity. 37 At that time she became ill and died. When they had washed her, they laid her in a room upstairs.

38 Since Lydda was near Joppa, the disciples, who heard that Peter was there, sent two men to him with the request, "Please come to us without delay." 39 So Peter got up and went with them; and when he arrived, they took him to the room upstairs. All the widows stood beside him, weeping and showing tunics and other clothing that Dorcas had made while she was with them. 40 Peter put all of them outside, and then he knelt down and prayed. He turned to the body and said, "Tabitha, get up." Then she opened her eyes, and seeing Peter, she sat up. 41 He gave her his hand and helped her up. Then calling the saints and widows, he showed her to be alive. 42 This became known throughout Joppa, and many believed in the Lord.

Sharing between Communities

Acts 11:27 At that time prophets came down from Jerusalem to Antioch. 28 One of them named Agabus stood up and predicted by the Spirit that there would be a severe famine over all the world; and this took place during the reign of Claudius. 29 The disciples determined that according to their ability, each would send relief to the believers living in Judea; 30 this they did, sending it to the elders by Barnabas and Saul.

The Great Baker

Matthew 13:33 . . . "The kingdom of heaven is like yeast that a woman took and mixed in with three measures of flour until all of it was leavened."

First Impression

5 minutes
Briefly mention a question you have about the reading or one thing in it that surprised, impressed, delighted, or challenged you. No discussion! Just listen to one another's reactions.

Exploring the Theme

If participants have not read this section already, read it aloud. Otherwise go on to "Questions for Reflection and Discussion."

Acts 2:41–47. Peter's sermon has a tremendous impact. Thousands of men and women are struck by the truth of his message about Jesus' death and resurrection. Seeking baptism, they flood into the Christian community like a rain-swollen stream pouring into a small pond.

Jesus is no longer physically present with his followers. But he is everywhere behind the scenes in the suddenly expanded community of his followers, making his presence felt through the Holy Spirit. In fact, it seems Jesus is even more powerfully present than before his departure. Through the apostles, he continues to teach and heal. He continues to draw his followers to the table with himself, as he did repeatedly during his public life.

Sometimes their meals follow the pattern of his Last Supper. Through this celebration, he continues to make his saving death present to his followers and shares his risen self with them.

When the disciples asked Jesus about the coming of God's kingdom (Acts 1:6—Week 4), his somewhat puzzling answer was that they would receive the Holy Spirit, who would enable them to bear witness to him (1:7–8). Now, observing how the Spirit is acting through them, the disciples can see the connection between their testimony and the coming of God's kingdom. People who believe their testimony about Jesus experience God's kingdom by being baptized, receiving God's forgiveness, and taking part in the grace-filled life of the Christian community. During his ministry, Jesus made God's kingdom available to people through his own presence. Now God's kingdom is available to people in the community of Jesus' followers.

The signs of God's kingdom are not limited to the healings the apostles perform (2:43). The whole body of believers reflects the presence of God's kingdom by their care for one another. Guided by the Spirit, the believers put Jesus' instructions in Mark 8 and 10 into practice: they become servants of one another. They treat their possessions as blessings entrusted to them for the good of those who need them. A Spirit-inspired recognition of solidarity begins to overcome their ordinary selfishness and possessiveness.

A new society is appearing in the midst of the old, marked by the social justice that God desires.

"They would sell their possessions," Luke tells us, and give the proceeds to the poor (2:45). They *would* do it—not all at once, but from time to time. Apparently not all of them actually sell their property; some keep their homes and open them to the community, since "they broke bread at home" (2:46), that is, in their homes.

The community meals in the larger homes of prosperous members serve many purposes: celebrating the Lord's Supper, teaching, getting to know one another, and providing nourishment for poorer members. The believers have no church buildings, offices, agencies, or institutions. All they have are their homes, so that is what they use.

Acts 4:32–37. Luke lets one man's generosity illustrate what many members of the Christian community did. Barnabas sells his property to provide for those who are in need. He is Ahab and Jezebel in reverse.

Again (compare 2:44) Luke tells us that the Christians hold their property in common. He seems to mean a mentality rather than a legal arrangement. If the owners had legally placed their properties in common, they would no longer be able to sell them, as Barnabas does. The members consider their possessions as no longer their own, that is, they are at the service of the community. The property owners have changed their minds about their possessions: each says to himself or herself, "This is no longer *mine;* it belongs to Jesus and is to be used for his purposes." (Consider writing *that* on the cover of your checkbook!)

"There was not a needy person among them" (4:34). Now there is a remarkable statement. At this time, many people in Jerusalem are poor. Certainly many of the Christians in Jerusalem are poor. Yet none of the believers lacks the basics of life. Our readings in Week 2 contained instructions to lend freely to needy neighbors (Leviticus 25:35–37). The believers go one better: they give what they have to those in need.

All this sharing and caring goes on *within* the Christian community. This is not because the Christians care only about their own. As Luke shows, they are making every effort to bring into their community everyone they can. But they recognize a special bond with fellow disciples of Jesus (compare Mark 10:28–30).

In caring for needy people, they take the main approach open to them, given the limitations of first-century society. Households are the basic social units. The way to care for a needy person is to bring him or her into the network of relationships—involving relatives, slaves, clients, freed slaves, and employees—centered on a household. One cannot take a child abandoned on the street to an orphanage, for there are none; but one can bring the child home. Luke shows the Christian community in Jerusalem developing into a network of households, each a center of Christian life where people in need find friendship and help. This household-based approach to Christian life and service became so characteristic of the early Christians that New Testament writers refer to the Church as the household of God (see Ephesians 2:19; 1 Timothy 3:5; 1 Peter 4:17).

Acts 6:1–7. Rather than giving the impoverished widows a handout of food or money, the Christians are apparently inviting them to meals in their homes. This is implied by the fact that the "distribution" for them is "daily" (6:1). Members of the community with material resources are treating the widows as nonresidential members of their households.

A problem with this arrangement arises in the Greek-speaking section of the Christian community. The apostles do not wish to become directly involved in the problem, not because they regard caring for widows as unimportant (if they thought that, they would not assemble the whole community to deal with the problem) but because they must keep to their assignment, which involves public preaching about Jesus. Apparently, the community entrusts the situation to some very promising leaders, since two of them—Stephen and Philip—are soon acting just like the apostles (Acts 7–8, compare chapters 3–4). This indicates the priority the Christian community places on caring for the needy. As a parallel, imagine a bishop putting a highly trained and talented priest in charge not of the diocesan seminary but of the local soup kitchen.

Luke holds up the Jerusalem community as a model. But he lets us see that these first Christians have not achieved instant perfection (see also 5:1–11).

Acts 9:36–42. Tabitha is financially comfortable. She has a two-story house (9:37), money to buy fabric, and the leisure to make clothes for needy neighbors. Perhaps her house is a center of Christian life in Joppa (near Tel Aviv, in Israel). Peter's raising her to life is an amazing sign of God's power. Yet Tabitha's life was already remarkable. As a "disciple" of Jesus, she was "devoted to good works and acts of charity" (9:36). Miracles have a place in the Church, but Tabitha's lifestyle will be more important in the long run.

Acts 11:27–30. Our final episode shows the early Christians sharing their material resources not only within each local community but also between one community and another.

Reflections. The Holy Spirit made a deep impact on the first Christians. Their commitment to each other stands as an encouragement as to what the Spirit can do among us, also.

Acts does not, however, give us a model for how to contribute to justice in society beyond the boundaries of the Church. Such broader efforts were out of the reach of the first Christians— and remained out of Christians' reach until governments recognized Christianity as legal. For three centuries, Christians were limited to working on the personal level. Once Christianity became legal in the Mediterranean world, Christians began to affect their societies in numerous ways—influencing government policies, shaping popular customs, developing institutions for social services (schools, orphanages, hospitals), teaching morality and principles of social justice. Results have varied greatly. In some cases, Christians have made a profound impression on their societies, ameliorating social evils and giving rise to a more humane civilization.

A strikingly apt image for this process was provided by Jesus himself. Christians have been like yeast in dough (Matthew 13:33). Yeast works from within. Christians did not begin with a grand plan for social transformation. They began by following Jesus in their circumstances. At first they were a powerless and tiny minority. But over time, their effects on societies around the world have been great and continue today.

Questions for Reflection and Discussion

45 minutes
Choose questions according to your interest and time.

1 If you had lived in Jerusalem at the time of our readings from Acts, would you have been inclined to join the Christians?

2 Luke writes that God added those who were being saved to the Christian community (2:47). What does this imply about the connection between experiencing life in Christ and participating in the Church?

3 The first Christians showed a special concern for the needs of fellow believers. Do Christians today have a special responsibility for fellow Christians in need?

4 Reread Acts 2:43–47 and 4:32–35. What seems to be the relationship between the richness of the Jerusalem Christians' community life and the effectiveness of the apostles' preaching about Jesus? What can Acts teach us about the relationship between Christians' efforts for social justice and the effectiveness of our evangelization?

5 Look back to the readings in Week 1 and reread Matthew 13:33 in this week's readings. What images or comparisons for God do these readings suggest? Taken together, what picture of God do these readings communicate?

6 In what ways can Christians use their homes today in service to people with various needs?

7 In what ways could parishes and Christian groups today learn from the way the Christians in Jerusalem cared for each other?

8 What significance might the episode in Acts 11:27–30 have for Christians today?

9 Read Matthew 13:33 again. Is your life yeast in the dough? How could you be more yeasty?

10 **Focus Question.** Luke shows that the Christians' care for needy members in the community in Jerusalem was only part of their life together (Acts 2:41–47). What were the other elements? How important were these other elements for sustaining their care for each other? What conclusions could you draw for Christians' efforts for social justice today?

Prayer to Close

10 minutes
Use this approach—or create your own!

◆ Let one person read aloud
Matthew 25:31–46. Pause for
silent reflection. Allow time for
any who wish to express brief
prayers regarding anything that
has been read and reflected on
in the course of the six weeks.
Ask one member of the group
to offer a prayer on behalf of
the whole group, asking for
God's help to respond to his
word. Close together with an
Our Father.

Saints in the Making

Finding Christ in the Chaos

This section is a supplement for individual reading.

In 1936, New York was "in the depths of the Depression," as people used to say. After seven years of business downturn and high unemployment, many people were simply destitute—homeless, and in many cases, hopeless. But those in lower Manhattan could find a meal, and some hope, at a House of Hospitality operated by the Catholic Worker—an organization with big ideas and just about as few resources as the people it served.

Under the leadership of its founder, a sometime newspaperwoman named Dorothy Day, the House of Hospitality served meals and gave shelter in a minimal fashion to homeless people, volunteer staff, visitors, and others of indeterminate purpose. The Catholic Worker's ideal was to receive all as Christ. Since Dorothy Day and the other Catholic Worker staff were not keen on rules and regulations, order was at a minimum. Many of those who came seeking hospitality were troubled and troubling, so there were frictions. A staffer once joked that the House of Hospitality might better be called "the house of hostility." The same staffer also observed that "the test of a true Catholic Worker was if one could put up with bedbugs."

A visitor recalled that "it would be hard to invent a more motley group of men and women. Rich and poor, young and old, notable and humble felt welcome. At meals, an eminent French philosopher or a Brazilian prelate might be seated beside a Bowery alcoholic or a mentally confused woman who thinks the drinking water is poisoned." If there can be such a thing as holy chaos, the Catholic Worker hospitality house was it. Yet in this chaos, some people who had never heard of the social teaching of the Catholic Church (or of Acts 2:44–47) made contact with it in a concrete if jarring fashion.

Alongside the soup kitchen, Dorothy Day and the group's cofounder, Peter Maurin, published a newspaper, hosted an endless series of formal and informal lectures, and talked and talked. They hoped to spur people to radical thinking about social change—radical in rejecting materialism, in embracing love as the most powerful human dynamic, in recognizing Christ as the center of all.

For six decades, Dorothy Day was strenuously involved in the Catholic Worker and various social causes. She died in 1980.

Suggestions for Bible Discussion Groups

Like a camping trip, a Bible discussion group works best if you agree on where you're going and how you intend to get there. Many groups use their first meeting to talk over such questions. Here is a checklist of issues, with bits of advice from people who have experience in Bible discussions. (A planning discussion will go more smoothly if the leaders have thought through the following issues beforehand.)

Agree on your purpose. Are you getting together to gain wisdom and direction for your lives? to finally get acquainted with the Bible? to support one another in following Christ? to encourage those who are exploring—or reexploring—the Church? for other reasons?

Agree on attitudes. For example: "We're all beginners here." "We're here to help one another understand and respond to God's word." "We're not here to offer counseling or direction to each other." "We want to read Scripture prayerfully." What do *you* wish to emphasize? Make it explicit!

Agree on ground rules. Barbara J. Fleischer, in her useful book *Facilitating for Growth,* recommends that a group clearly state its approach to the following:

- ◆ *Preparation.* Do we agree to read the material and prepare answers to the questions before each meeting?
- ◆ *Attendance.* What kind of priority will we give to our meetings?
- ◆ *Self-revelation.* Are we willing to gradually help the others in the group gradually get to know us—our weaknesses as well as our strengths, our needs as well as our gifts?
- ◆ *Listening.* Will we commit ourselves to listen to one another?
- ◆ *Confidentiality.* Will we keep everything that is shared with the group in the group?
- ◆ *Discretion.* Will we refrain from sharing about the faults and sins of people who are not in the group?
- ◆ *Encouragement and support.* Will we give as well as receive?
- ◆ *Participation.* Will we give each person the time and opportunity to make a contribution?

You could probably take a pen and draw a circle around *listening* and *confidentiality*. Those two points are especially important.

The following items could be added to Fleischer's list:

♦ *Relationship with parish.* Is our group part of the adult faith-formation program? independent but operating with the express approval of the pastor? not a parish-based group?

♦ *New members.* Will we let new members join us once we have begun the six weeks of discussions?

Agree on housekeeping.

♦ *When will we meet?*

♦ *How often will we meet?* Meeting weekly or every other week is best if you can manage it. William Riley remarks, "Meetings once a month are too distant from each other for the threads of the last session not to be lost" *(The Bible Study Group: An Owner's Manual).*

♦ *How long will each meeting run?*

♦ *Where will we meet?*

♦ *Is any setup needed?* Christine Dodd writes that "the problem with meeting in a place like a church hall is that it can be very soul-destroying" given the cold, impersonal feel of many church facilities. If you have to meet in a church facility, Dodd recommends doing something to make the area homey *(Making Scripture Work).*

♦ *Who will host the meetings?* Leaders and hosts are not necessarily the same people.

♦ *Will we have refreshments?* Who will provide them? Don Cousins and Judson Poling make this recommendation: "Serve refreshments if you like, but save snacks and other foods for the end of the meeting to minimize distractions" *(Leader's Guide 1).*

♦ *What about child care?* Most experienced leaders of Bible discussion groups discourage bringing infants or other children to adult Bible discussions.

Agree on leadership. You need someone to facilitate— to keep the discussion on track, to see that everyone has a chance to speak, to help the group stay on schedule. Rena Duff, editor of the newsletter *Sharing God's Word Today,* recommends having two or three people take turns leading the discussions.

It's okay if the leader is not an expert on the Bible. You have this Six Weeks book as a guide, and if questions come up that no one can answer, you can delegate a participant to do a little research between meetings. Perhaps someone on the pastoral staff of your parish could offer advice. Or help may be available from your diocesan catechetical office or a local Catholic college or seminary.

It's important for the leader to set an example of listening, to draw out the quieter members (and occasionally restrain the more vocal ones), to move the group on when it gets stuck, to get the group back on track when the discussion moves away from the topic, and to restate and summarize what the group is learning. Sometimes the leader needs to remind the members of their agreements. An effective group leader is enthusiastic about the topic and the discussions, sets an example of learning from others and of using resources for growing in understanding.

As a discussion group matures, other members of the group will increasingly share in doing all these things on their own initiative.

Bible discussion is an opportunity to experience the fulfillment of Jesus' promise "Where two or three are gathered in my name, I am there among them" (Matthew 18:20). Put your discussion group in Jesus' hands. Pray for the guidance of the Spirit. And have a great time exploring God's word together!

Y ou can use this booklet just as well for individual study as for group discussion. While discussing the Bible with other people can be a rich experience, there are advantages to reading on your own. For example:

◆ You can focus on the points that interest you most.

◆ You can go at your own pace.

◆ You can be completely relaxed and unashamedly honest in your answers to all the questions, since you don't have to share them with anyone!

My suggestions for using this booklet on your own are these:

◆ Don't skip "Questions to Begin" or "First Impression."

◆ Take your time on "Questions for Reflection and Discussion." While a group will probably not have enough time to work on all the questions, you can allow yourself the time to consider all of them if you are using the booklet by yourself.

◆ After reading "Exploring the Theme," go back and reread the Scripture text before doing the "Questions for Reflection and Discussion."

◆ Take the time to look up all the parenthetical Scripture references.

◆ Read additional sections of Scripture before and after the excerpts in this book. For example, read the portions of Scripture that come before and after the sections that form the readings in this Six Weeks book. You will understand the readings better by viewing them in context in the Bible.

◆ Since you control the pace, give yourself plenty of opportunities to reflect on the meaning of the Scripture passages for you. Let your reading be an opportunity for these words to become God's words to you.

Bibles

The following editions of the Bible contain the full set of biblical books recognized by the Catholic Church, along with a great deal of useful explanatory material:

- The Catholic Study Bible (Oxford University Press), which uses the text of the New American Bible
- The Catholic Bible: Personal Study Edition (Oxford University Press), which also uses the text of the New American Bible
- The New Jerusalem Bible, the regular (not the reader's) edition (Doubleday)

Books, Web Sites, and Other Resources

- *Tenth Anniversary Edition of Economic Justice for All* and other statements on social justice by the bishops of the United States, especially *"For I Was Hungry and You Gave Me Food"* and *Faithful Citizenship.* See www.nccbuscc.org/sdwp/index.htm.
- *Catechism of the Catholic Church.* On the supreme value of human life, legitimate defense, abortion, and other life issues: sections 2258–2330. On private property and the common good, respect for people and property, stewardship of the earth, and principles of social justice and solidarity: sections 2401–2463.
- *Raising Kids Who Will Make a Difference: Helping Your Family Live with Integrity, Value Simplicity, and Care for Others* by Susan V. Vogt (Chicago: Loyola Press, 2002).
- World Youth Alliance at www.worldyouthalliance.org.
- The Dominican Sisters of Hawthorne at www.hawthorne-dominicans.org.
- The Catholic Worker Movement at www.catholicworker.org.
- Catholic Relief Services at www.catholicrelief.org.
- Catholic Charities at www.catholiccharitiesusa.org.
- St. Vincent de Paul Society at www.svdpusa.com.